SALVATION

SALVATION
The Journey From Here To Eternity

KIM C. BROOKS, M.D.

XULON PRESS

Xulon Press
2301 Lucien Way #415
Maitland, FL 32751
407.339.4217
www.xulonpress.com

© 2023 by Kim C. Brooks, M.D.

All rights reserved solely by the author. The author guarantees all contents are original and do not infringe upon the legal rights of any other person or work. No part of this book may be reproduced in any form without the permission of the author.

Due to the changing nature of the Internet, if there are any web addresses, links, or URLs included in this manuscript, these may have been altered and may no longer be accessible. The views and opinions shared in this book belong solely to the author and do not necessarily reflect those of the publisher. The publisher therefore disclaims responsibility for the views or opinions expressed within the work.

Unless otherwise indicated, Scripture quotations taken from the Holy Bible, New International Version (NIV). Copyright © 1973, 1978, 1984, 2011 by Biblica, Inc.™. Used by permission. All rights reserved.

Scripture quotations taken from the Holy Bible, New Living Translation (NLT). Copyright ©1996, 2004, 2007 by Tyndale House Foundation. Used by permission of Tyndale House Publishers, Inc.

Scripture quotations taken from The Message (MSG). Copyright © 1993, 1994, 1995, 1996, 2000, 2001, 2002. Used by permission of NavPress Publishing Group. Used by permission. All rights reserved.

Scripture quotations taken from the New King James Version (NKJV). Copyright © 1982 by Thomas Nelson, Inc. Used by permission. All rights reserved.

Paperback ISBN-13: 978-1-66286-405-6
Ebook ISBN-13: 978-1-66286-406-3

Acknowledgments

First, giving honor to God for finding me in my skepticism and leading me to the light.

There are so many people who have nurtured me, fed me, and encouraged me along the way in my spiritual journey. I would like to thank Presiding Elder Dr. John Butler and Rev. Donna Butler; the members of Wesley Chapel A.M.E. Zion Church in Asheboro, NC; Mt. Airy and Chestnut A.M.E. Zion Churches in Mt. Gilead, North Carolina; and Zion Grove A.M.E. Zion Church in Eagle Springs, North Carolina. And a special thank you to the members of Greater Warner Tabernacle A.M.E. Zion Church in Knoxville, Tennessee who supported me as the pastor's wife and encouraged me during the early stages of my ministry. To Bishop Darryl B. Starnes and Missionary Supervisor Camille C. Starnes, thank you for being examples of godly leadership.

I would also like to thank my daughters, Devyn, and Lauren, who quietly endured my struggles as a working mother trying to find the balance between family and work. And a special blessing to my son, Jayden. Even though he cannot speak, he has "preached" many a sermon and continues to be a quiet source of inspiration for me.

And most importantly, I would like to thank my husband and my pastor, Cleo, for his love, friendship, mentorship, guidance, and above all, his unwavering support and willingness to speak the truth. I thank God for bringing us together and blessing me with exactly what I needed in a spouse.

TABLE OF CONTENTS

Acknowledgments v
The First Step ix
Introduction xiii

Chapter 1   So, You're Saved. Now What? 1
Chapter 2   Learning about God 9
Chapter 3   What Kind of Relationship Do You
            Want to Have with God? 23
Chapter 4   The Benefits of a Living Faith 28
Chapter 5   How to Love Like God 41
Chapter 6   God's Love in Action 48
Chapter 7   Fear or Faith? 52
Chapter 8   Why Do Bad Things Happen to
            Good People? 61
Chapter 9   Sharing What You Have Learned 78
Chapter 10 Worshiping in Spirit and Truth 84
Chapter 11 Created to Serve 89
Chapter 12 Caring for Your Soul 93

The First Step

Romans 10:8-10 (NIV) encourages us:

> But what does it say? "The word is near you; it is in your mouth and in your heart," that is, the word of faith we are proclaiming:
>
> That if you confess with your mouth, "Jesus is Lord," and believe in your heart that God raised him from the dead, you will be saved.
>
> For it is with your heart that you believe and are justified, and it is with your mouth that you confess and are saved.

A journey of a thousand miles begins with the first step. A child learning to walk begins with the first step and entering into right relationship with God begins with the first step. You are invited to take a journey of faith. It is as simple as following the steps below:

1. You must be willing to acknowledge the state you are in; this comes with confession. We are all sinners. By confessing our sins to God, we mitigate sin's power over our lives. The Word of God tells us there

is power in the tongue. You can speak good, and you can speak evil. Which do you desire to speak into your life? If you are sincere in your desire to be in relationship with God, then open your mouth and speak the words: "Jesus is my Lord and Savior."
2. Believe in your heart. A belief in the heart is not just a thought, but a belief in your spirit. A belief dwells deep in your inner being. You must believe that God so loved the world that He gave His only Son, Jesus Christ, for us and raised Him from the dead.
3. By confessing your sins and believing in Jesus Christ as your Lord and Savior, you are saved!

The journey to salvation begins with these first steps. But the journey should not end here. I use the term *journey* because salvation is the process that God uses to make you more like His Son, Jesus Christ. Whatever you want to call it—the road, the journey, or the race to salvation begins with the first step. The gift of God is eternal life, but it depends on how you run the race. The race is about fixing your eyes on Jesus, trusting Him, and obeying Him until the race is over. Paul tells us in 1 Corinthians 9:24–25 (NIV), "Run in such a way as to get the prize. Everyone who competes in the games goes into strict training. They do it to get a crown that will not last, but we *[believers]* do it to get a crown that will last forever."

So, I invite you to take the first step on the most important journey of your life—the journey of faith in Jesus Christ.

Believe

Psalm 107:2 (NIV) says, "Let the redeemed of the Lord tell their story."

This is my story.

Introduction

When I accepted Jesus Christ as my Lord and Savior, I expected salvation to change me overnight. I soon realized that my expectations of salvation were incorrect. What I discovered is that salvation is not an isolated event, but a journey, and my salvation story is no exception. My story is not just about one event or point in time. Instead, it is many points and events in my life that have occurred over many years, and it is comprised of many different encounters with God over time. My salvation story is about my journey from skepticism to belief. My hope is that the story of my salvation journey will be an inspiration to others.

    I was not raised in church. I can remember going to church perhaps a handful of times as a child. Attending church and learning about God were not stressed in our home. During my high school years, I attended a church youth group because I had friends who belonged to the youth group. At that time, I felt no connection to God and had no desire to be in relationship with Him. For me, the youth group was simply another opportunity for me to hang out with my friends. I didn't begin to wonder about God until I was an adult. After high school, I visited church a couple of times during college, but I never felt a connection to God at that time either. However, I felt like I should try to find out a little more about God just in case He really existed.

In college, I was just too busy to be concerned with God. As a scientist by nature, my life at that time was about what could or could not be proven. Besides, I was a biology major, working two jobs, participating in extracurricular activities, and trying to get into medical school. That did not leave me much time to cultivate a relationship with God. Matriculation into medical school was no exception. I was too busy learning about the intricacies of the human body, disease processes, and the medical treatment of disease to learn about the God that created the miraculous human body I was studying. It was during my OB/GYN residency in Pittsburgh, Pennsylvania that I started to attend church on a regular basis. I felt like something was missing in my life, and maybe that something was God. That is when my salvation journey started. There was a yearning in my heart, and I had a desire to learn more about God. I was full of questions about God and wanted meaningful answers to those questions.

I started to attend a nondenominational church in Pittsburgh. I can remember going to church Sunday after Sunday and staying in my seat when the invitation to Christian discipleship was given. Even though I could feel the tug on my heart, I hesitated to respond. A friend would go with me to church most Sundays. I think I was too embarrassed to go to the altar and give my life to Christ when she was with me. On the Sunday I finally decided to accept Christ, I had gone to church alone that day. The call was so strong that I couldn't get to the altar fast enough. I accepted Jesus Christ as my Lord and Savior that day in 1995.

Once at the altar, I made the confession that Jesus Christ is Lord. I started to attend Bible study and began to learn more about God. But, after being saved, I struggled in

Introduction

my relationship with God. I can remember multiple people talking to me about having a personal relationship with God, but I just couldn't figure out how to make my relationship with God personal. I had made the confession that Jesus was Lord, and I wanted to believe. I just didn't know how. What was I doing wrong?

Several months after accepting Christ, I met the man who would become my husband, Cleo Brooks, Jr. He grew up in church, and his father was a pastor. Together, we started to attend church on a regular basis. Just as I was starting to become comfortable in church, I finished my residency. In what would be a glimpse of our future frenetic life together, in the span of four weeks, I finished residency, took my board exam, got married, bought a house, and moved to Rocky Mount, North Carolina. It took us a while to find a church in Rocky Mount that felt like somewhere we could grow spiritually. Shortly after finding that church, I resigned from my job, and we moved to Asheboro, North Carolina. Once again, we found ourselves looking for a new church home. We visited several churches in the area until we finally decided that Wesley Chapel A.M.E. Zion Church in Asheboro would become our new church home. Between moving from Rocky Mount to Asheboro, God blessed us with our daughter Devyn. And after getting settled in Asheboro, we were blessed again with our daughter Lauren. A couple of years later, we decided to expand our family and we were blessed with our son, Jayden.

As our family grew, we became more committed to attending church regularly. Wesley Chapel was a spirit-filled church with a spirit-filled pastor and provided the perfect environment to nurture me as a fledgling Christian. Eventually, we attended Sunday worship service, Bible study, and Sunday school on a regular basis. But, I was still struggling with how to have a personal relationship with God. As I was struggling with that, my husband was wrestling with the call that had been placed on his life for the ministry. He finally admitted to me one day that God wanted him to do something, but he never really admitted to the call that God had placed on his life many years before. Little did we know that our lives and our relationship with God were about to change.

On Thursday, July 24, 2003, my life, and my relationship with God, would change forever. I happened to be off work that day because I was scheduled to work the weekend. I volunteered to give a talk at the local Boys and Girls Club that day, which was right next door to my daycare. I got the kids dressed, fed them breakfast, and thought nothing of dropping them off at daycare as usual. I made my way over to the Boys and Girls Club and was in the middle of my talk when I got an emergency page from the daycare. I excused myself and ran next door. When I got there, I was told my son, Jayden, had choked on a grape and was taken to the hospital by ambulance.

I jumped in my car and raced to the hospital as fast as I could. The entire drive to the hospital I expected to find a screaming child looking for his mother. I let myself into the staff entrance of the emergency department and asked the secretary where they had taken the baby that had just arrived by ambulance. She pointed to trauma bay one. I ran to the trauma bay and pulled back the curtain only to find them doing CPR on my infant son. Words cannot describe the utter shock and disbelief I felt. I knew immediately things were bad—and I knew immediately that Jayden had a brain injury.

Unlike adults, children can only go a few minutes without oxygen before they go into complete cardiopulmonary arrest.

Introduction

The fact that the doctors were still doing CPR meant Jayden had been deprived of oxygen for a long time. I started crying and became quite distraught in the middle of the emergency department. I called Cleo to tell him that Jayden was in the emergency department. Cleo worked in the hospital as a social worker and was only a few floors away, but it seemed like forever before he arrived.

The ED staff had always known me to be calm and collected. I was never one of those physicians that expressed panic, even if I was feeling it inside. I was hysterical, and the ED staff didn't know what to do with me. Cleo tried to comfort me, but I was still standing in the middle of the emergency department and I was wailing uncontrollably. Someone finally ushered us to a small family waiting area where we waited and waited. It was an area separate from the rest of the emergency waiting area. It was usually reserved for having difficult discussions with family members—discussions that were not appropriate for the open areas of the ED.

Our pastor, Reverend John Butler, and his wife, Donna, came and waited with us. We waited and we prayed, and we prayed, and we waited. Eventually, we received word that after Jayden choked on the grape, there had been some difficulty getting the grape out of his windpipe. Despite their best efforts, the daycare workers were unable to dislodge the grape. It was a police officer who arrived on the scene ten minutes later and dislodged the grape. The ten minutes without oxygen and forty-five minutes without a pulse or blood pressure led to a severe brain injury. I tried to express to Cleo the gravity of Jayden's situation, but I don't think he really understood the severity of his condition until later that evening. As a physician, I knew that ten minutes without oxygen and even longer without a pulse meant a debilitating brain injury.

The doctors and nurses at our local hospital worked feverishly to restore Jayden's pulse and blood pressure. By the time I saw him again, he was intubated, on a ventilator, and had a tube coming out of almost every orifice in his body. It was horrendous seeing my child in that state. Our local hospital was a small community hospital that was not equipped to deal with such a seriously ill child. The decision was made to transfer Jayden to the nearest children's hospital in Winston-Salem, North Carolina. While we waited on the transport team to arrive, we were joined by the partners in my practice and members of my office staff. We formed a circle in the waiting room, joined hands, and prayed. I was still in shock. It felt like someone had kicked me in the stomach and ripped out my intestines. How could this happen to my eleven-month-old baby?

Cleo stayed in Asheboro to make overnight arrangements for our daughters who were still at the daycare. He would join me in Winston-Salem later that evening. During the fifty-minute ride from the hospital in Asheboro to Brenner's Children's Hospital in Winston-Salem, North Carolina, I thought I knew my child's fate. As I rode in the front seat of the ambulance, I thought my son was going to be brain dead and end up as an organ donor. I could not get the thought of my son being an organ donor out of my mind. The ambulance driver tried to console me but to no avail. I was a slobbering, tearful mess.

After arriving at Brenner's Children's Hospital, the doctors assessed Jayden and stabilized his condition. The doctor who talked to me confirmed my fears. He told me things I already knew—that Jayden was critically ill and had suffered a profound brain injury. He explained that

Introduction

after being deprived of oxygen for so long, Jayden's brain would begin to swell from the injury, and there would not be enough room in his skull for his swollen brain. His brain would then herniate into the hole in his skull where the spine joins the skull, and this would lead to brain death. Once that happens, the brain would no longer function and the only thing keeping the person alive would be the ventilator. The doctor was concerned Jayden would not survive the night. And, if he did survive the night, his prognosis was bleak at best.

Cleo arrived at the hospital later that evening. By then, the doctors had changed shifts, and it was a different doctor who spoke to us about our very sick little boy. Together, we received the same report from the second doctor that I received from the first one. Jayden may not live through the night. He explained the first twenty-four hours were critical. It was devastating news. Hearing those words sent us into a tailspin. Once we calmed down, we called our family and friends for prayer and support. Soon, we had an army of family and friends with us to provide support on what was just the beginning of a very long journey with our son. We continued to pray and receive reports from the doctors and nurses about Jayden's condition. The first twenty-four hours came and went with no signs of brain death, and he remained in critical condition.

On Friday night, my mother came to visit. Her visit stretched into the early hours of Saturday morning. She visited with Jayden, prayed for him, and prayed for us as well. After praying, she asked if we were saved. Cleo responded with, "Not like I should be." So right there in the hospital waiting room, we both said the sinner's prayer and received Jesus Christ as our Lord and Savior. That was not the first

Salvation

time I had prayed that prayer, and it was not the first time I had accepted Jesus Christ as my Lord and Savior.

As she was preparing to go home, she mentioned to me that I should not let anything get in the way of my son's blessings. I thought long and hard about her statement. It finally occurred to me what had prevented me from establishing a personal relationship with God in the past. *It was my pride.* I had been too proud to fully give myself to God and too worried about what other people might think of me if I confessed Jesus as my Lord and Savior. After all, I was a doctor and a science-minded individual. My life was about what I could prove and about facts. At that time, God was not something I could prove. I believed in God, but I was still holding back.

After she left, we went back to Jayden's room in the ICU, and I began to pray over him. It was during that prayer that I finally surrendered myself to God and let go of the pride that had been in the way. I finally confessed that I no longer cared what other people thought. It was then that God's Holy Spirit came over me like a mighty rushing wind. As I yielded to the Spirit, an amazing joy came over me, and I began to leap and shout right there in the hospital room. God's Spirit touched me in such a way that I could never doubt or deny his existence again. After my encounter with God's Spirit, a peace came over me that baffled our friends and my colleagues who came to visit us. It was like God picked us up and carried us through that traumatic experience.

Cleo accepted his call to the ministry during Jayden's hospital stay. Despite what appeared to be a catastrophe, God used the situation for good. I can't say I would ever ask for something like this to happen, but I recognize the good that has resulted from it. The good that resulted was only because we surrendered to God and allowed Him to work in our lives. God was there to offer His love, His peace, His comfort, and His strength, and we accepted. I've seen far too many families torn apart by situations like these. By allowing God to work in our lives, we were able to face things we never could have faced alone.

Jayden spent a month at the children's hospital. He was then transferred to a rehabilitation hospital in Charlotte, North Carolina, where he spent another month in intensive therapy. While there, we learned the difficult tasks required to care for Jayden on a daily basis. Despite what the doctors had said, the swelling of his brain never resulted in brain death. His accident, however, left him severely impaired. My son has never walked or talked and still cannot walk or talk to this day. He cannot eat or drink. He has a tracheostomy (a hole in his trachea) that allows him to breathe and a feeding tube in his stomach for his daily nourishment and water. And he requires round-the-clock care.

After Jayden's accident, the Asheboro community embraced us and showered us with love. We received an abundance of cards, letters, phone calls, and food. It seemed as if the entire community was praying for us. I would send very specific prayer requests to the community, they would pray, and God would answer our prayers. For example, the doctors told us Jayden would never be able to survive without a ventilator because his breathing was too erratic. We prayed for his breathing to become more regular and he came off the ventilator.

Not only did I ask for prayer for Jayden, but I also asked for prayer for the daycare workers. The workers were in anguish and wracked with guilt over Jayden's accident. They needed prayer as much as we did. I have often been asked if we sued the daycare over Jayden's accident. We chose not to sue the daycare. It was, after all, an accident. What we needed, what the daycare needed, and what the community needed was forgiveness. Instead of suing, we chose to forgive them because that is what God requires of us. Ephesians 4:32 (NLT) tells us, "Instead, be kind to each other, tenderhearted, forgiving one another, just as God through Christ has forgiven you." And what many people consider unbelievable is that we continued to send our daughters to the same daycare until they went to kindergarten. I know it's hard for people to understand our actions. How could you forgive someone that allowed that to happen to your child? Why would you send your children back to the same daycare? My answer is this—when God showers you with His love, forgiveness is one of the natural outcomes.

I would love to tell you that Jayden recovered from his injury without any mental or physical deficits, but that is not the case. But I know that God is not finished with him yet. By all accounts, our son should have been brain dead and should have died. But God meant for him to survive. I know this because when he was born, the soft spot in his skull that allows the baby's head to fit through the birth canal was huge. I remember asking the pediatrician about it the day after he was born. The soft spot on the top of his head was so large it extended all the way into his forehead. The pediatrician was not concerned and explained the soft spot would close as he grew. I didn't give it a second thought until much later. It was this very large soft spot that gave him the extra space in his skull to prevent his brain from herniating when it swelled. The large soft spot did not prevent the brain injury, but it did prevent brain death and allowed him to survive.

Introduction

Let me make one thing perfectly clear. I do not believe that God orchestrated the event that happened to our son. God was not trying to get our attention and was not trying to teach us a lesson. What happened was an accident, but God was there for us when we needed Him the most. It was our willingness to open our lives to Him that resulted in the peace and the strength we needed to get through that situation. I think Philippians 4:7 (NIV) describes the peace that comforted us during that tumultuous time in our lives. "And the peace of God, which transcends all understanding, will guard your hearts and your minds in Christ Jesus."

Jayden's accident is just part of my salvation journey. Without that part of the journey, I am not sure what kind of relationship I would have with God. But, my journey is not over. And I can't wait to see what else God has in store for us. Good, bad, or indifferent, I know God will be with us every step of the way.

Chapter 1

So, You're Saved. Now What?

Congratulations on your decision to accept Jesus Christ into your life! You are about to embark on the most fascinating, bewildering, and fulfilling journey of your life. Salvation is just that—a journey. For most of us, salvation does not bring about an overnight transformation. The transformation is a gradual change that occurs as we learn more and more about God and apply the things we have learned to our lives. Second Corinthians 5:17 (NKJV) tells us, "Therefore, if anyone *is* in Christ, *he is* a new creation; old things have passed away; behold, all things have become new." As we learn about God, we grow. The more we learn about God, the more we learn to trust Him. The more we learn to trust God, the more we want to obey God.

When Jesus was asked which is the greatest commandment, Matthew 22: 37-39 (NIV) tells us:

> Jesus replied: "Love the Lord your God with all your heart and with all your soul and with all your mind." This is the first and greatest commandment. And the second is like it: "Love your neighbor as yourself."

But in John 13:34 (NIV), Jesus commands even more of us, "A new command I give you: Love one another. As I have loved you, so you must love one another."

God commands us to love one another as He loves us. This is not an easy task. It is when we learn to love like God that we become transformed into the new creation He desires us to be. First John 4:12 (NIV) tells us, "No one has ever seen God; but if we love one another, God lives in us, and his love is made complete in us." It is through our relationship with God that we learn what love is. It is love that changes us and the world around us.

So, what is the next step in your journey? The next step is to learn about God because God knows all about you! He knows your struggles, strengths, weaknesses, joy, and pain. Jeremiah 1:5 (NIV) states, "Before I formed you in the womb I knew you, before you were born I set you apart." Now it is time for you to learn about God for yourself.

A crucial part of any relationship is communication. We communicate with God through scripture and through prayer. Your relationship with God should be intimate, personal, and not solely based on what someone has told you. We should learn about God's Word through the committed reading of the Bible. My recommendation is to pick a translation of the Bible that you can understand, such as the *New Living Translation, New International Version, New King James Version,* or the *New Revised Standard Version* (just to name a few). Although there are many Bible reading plans and apps that will enable you to read the Bible in six months, a year, or even two years, I encourage you to read the Bible at your own pace. The salvation journey is a marathon, not a sprint. It is more important that you understand God's Word and how it applies to your life than completing a task on a checklist. A study Bible or a good Bible commentary will help you understand the background behind the scriptures and give you a deeper understanding of the Word of God.

Second, there is nothing more important on this journey than a rich prayer life. Prayer is your opportunity to speak to God, but prayer is also about God speaking to you. God speaks to us in whispers. First Kings 19: 11-12 (NIV) speaks of the "gentle whisper" of the Lord to the prophet Elijah. If we are distracted by the noisy world we live in, we can often miss God's messages to us. Your prayer time should be in a quiet, secluded place free from distractions. This should be a time for you to talk openly and honestly with God and wait for a response from Him.

The third part of establishing a meaningful relationship with God involves the Holy Spirit. In John 14:16-17 (NIV), Jesus promises the Holy Spirit who would be "Another advocate to help you and be with you forever—the Spirit of truth. ... But you know him, for he lives with you and will be in you." God is a spirit who is alive and well and very much a part of the world in which we live. The Spirit of God wants to become a part of you. His Spirit wants to live and breathe inside of you.

God has knocked on the door of your heart, and you have answered the door. Now it is time to invite God's Spirit into your heart. The continuation of your salvation journey is predicated on inviting the Holy Spirit into your life daily. Think of the Holy Spirit as your conscience, your moral compass, and your ever-constant travel companion. John 14:26 (NIV) describes the role of the Holy Spirit. "But the Advocate, the Holy Spirit, whom the Father will send in my name, will teach you all things and will remind you of everything I have said to you." However, you must renew and affirm the connection with the Holy Spirit on a daily basis. It is as simple as saying, "Lord, I invite your Holy Spirit to lead me and guide me today."

I know this all seems like a huge commitment. But trust me, any time invested in your relationship with God will be richly rewarded. Understand that God's rewards are different from what the world views as a reward. God's rewards as outlined in Galatians 5:22 (NIV 1984) include "love, joy, peace, patience, kindness, goodness, faithfulness, gentleness and self-control." How many of us have longed for peace in the middle of the turmoil and chaos in our lives? Building a strong relationship with God through reading scripture, prayer, and an intimate rapport with the Holy Spirit can provide you with unparalleled strength, peace, and joy in the middle of life's many struggles.

When I think of the many times that my relationship with God has helped me through life's struggles, there is one situation that will always stand out in my mind. Seven months after the incident that left him severely disabled, Jayden got sick and had been sick for several days. He was having difficulty breathing and needed oxygen to maintain adequate levels of oxygen in his blood. Eventually, I called an ambulance because we didn't have enough oxygen at home to meet his needs and breathing was becoming more difficult for him. When we got to the hospital, he was diagnosed with pneumonia and admitted to the intensive care unit.

Our local hospital did not have a pediatric intensive care unit. So, when Jayden got sick, he was admitted to the adult ICU. We finally got settled in the ICU in the middle of the night. When his pediatrician came to see him on her morning rounds, his breathing was improved, and he required minimal amounts of oxygen. Being cautious, she wanted to watch him a little longer. But, if he was still doing well at lunchtime, he could go home. Well, between 8 a.m. and lunchtime, he took a dramatic turn for the worse. He required a ventilator to help him breathe, but even with the ventilator, he was not able to maintain adequate levels of oxygen in his blood. He needed to be transferred to another hospital.

After making several calls all over the state, his pediatrician finally found a bed for him at the pediatric ICU at UNC Hospitals in Chapel Hill, North Carolina— an hour and a half from our home. His pediatrician wanted him transferred by helicopter because of his critical condition, but the helicopter was not available. UNC Hospitals sent a transport team by ambulance. When the transport team arrived, they worked feverishly to stabilize his condition, but they had significant difficulty. The transport team was concerned Jayden would not survive the ninety-minute ride to Chapel Hill by ambulance in his current condition. Amazingly, the helicopter became available and made its way to our small town in North Carolina. The transport team was still not able to stabilize him but now that the helicopter was there, they decided to transport him in his unstable condition. There was no room in the helicopter for me or my husband, so we watched the helicopter take off with our critically ill little boy.

We made the ninety-minute drive to Chapel Hill, praying that God's will be done for Jayden understanding that God's will may mean his death. We arrived at UNC Hospitals, not knowing whether Jayden was alive or dead. We finally found the pediatric ICU, anxious to see him, only to be told to remain in the waiting room. The voice on the intercom told us the doctor would come out to speak with us. We were given no indication of his condition and still didn't know if Jayden was alive or dead. We waited for quite a while. Finally, the doctor came out and spoke with us.

We were informed that we had a very sick little boy, and the next few hours would be critical. That was not the first or the last time a physician would give us a report like that about Jayden. The doctor escorted us to Jayden's room, which was filled with a plethora of medical equipment that was keeping him alive. He was paralyzed and heavily sedated to give him the best chance of survival. We prayed for him, and then we went to the sleep room that was provided for us adjacent to the ICU. We decided we were going to put the situation in God's hands, and we went to sleep. We slept well until about 4 a.m. when a scuffle in an adjoining room necessitated a visit from hospital security. After the scuffle, we went back to sleep.

We woke up early enough to be in Jayden's room before the doctors made their morning rounds. We learned from the nurse that Jayden had a good night and though his condition was still critical, it had improved. The doctor, however, could not believe the improvement and felt compelled to show us his chest x-rays so we could see the significant change that occurred in just a few hours. Gradually, Jayden continued to improve.

He spent almost two weeks in the ICU but stayed in the hospital for an entire month.

Only the kind of peace that God can provide allowed us to sleep that night when our son was knocking on death's door for the second time in his young life. Although it was still early for me in my salvation journey, I was still able to reap the extraordinary benefits of my relationship with God. I found peace in the middle of a storm.

Are you ready to continue your journey with God? Are you truly interested in a fulfilling relationship with God? If so, dedicate your time and energy to establishing a meaningful relationship with God by reading your Bible, praying, and inviting the Holy Spirit into your heart.

NOTES

Chapter 2

LEARNING ABOUT GOD

Like any relationship, the success of your relationship with God is dependent on how well you know each other and how well you communicate with each other. God knows all about you. He has even numbered the hairs on your head (Matthew 10:30, NIV). Now you need to learn about God. We learn about God by reading His Word, through our experiences with Him, and by communicating with Him in prayer.

The first thing you need to understand is the concept of the Trinity. The Trinity describes the three aspects of God. There is God the Father, God the Son, known to us as Jesus Christ, and God the Holy Spirit (or Holy Ghost). They are three, but they are also one. The Trinity describes God's relationship with God's self. First John 5:7 (NKJV) tells us, "For there are three that bear witness in heaven: the Father, the Word *(Jesus)*, and the Holy Spirit; and these three are one." Just as we have a mind, a body, and a spirit that are in relationship with one another; God the Father, God the Son, and God the Spirit are in relationship with one another. Just as our mind, body, and spirit work together to make us one being, God the Father, God the Son, and God the Holy Spirit are in unison with each other.

God knows all about our mind, our body, and our spirit. We must get to know the different aspects of God. God the Father is described in the Bible as "I Am" (Exodus 3:14, NIV). To me, that means God the Father can be anything and everything. He is the Creator (Genesis 1:1, NIV), the Beginning and the End (Revelation 22:13, NIV), and anything else I need Him to be. God the Son became flesh to pay the ransom for my sins. He is described in the Bible as Wonderful Counselor (Isaiah 9:6, NIV), Prince of Peace (Isaiah 9:6, NIV), the Messiah (Luke 2:11, NIV), the Son of God (Mark 1:1, KJV), and the Lamb of God (John 1:36, NIV). And God the Holy Spirit is described as the Comforter (John 14:16, KJV), the Advocate (John 14:26, NIV), and the Spirit of Truth (John 15:26, NIV). Each aspect of God desires to be in relationship with you. So how do you learn about God? It starts with reading God's Word.

Reading God's Word

As I look back over my salvation journey, my biggest struggle at the beginning of the journey was figuring out how to make my relationship with God personal. I was going to church, and I was reading my Bible occasionally, but I had difficulty understanding what I was reading. Finally, I bought a study Bible written in everyday language I could understand. The study Bible gave me background information and explained the scriptures in a way that made God's Word easier to understand. I was then able to understand how God's Word is relevant to my everyday life.

You should read your Bible for understanding, not just to check off your to-do list. To get a full understanding of God's Word, we must read critically. Most study Bibles will give an introduction that provides information about the author of the book, the general theme, and the historical background of the time period. This is important information that will give you a better understanding of the scripture. I encourage you to read the introduction to each book as well as the footnotes throughout the chapter. This information will provide context that will help you to better understand the scriptures. While reading, you should try to answer the following questions:

1. Who is speaking?
2. To whom are they speaking?
3. Why are they speaking?
4. What does this scripture mean to me?
5. How is this scripture relevant to me today?

It can also be helpful to read a passage in more than one translation. With the advent of the electronic Bible and Bible apps, multiple translations of the Bible are readily available. Reading a passage in multiple translations can give you a better understanding of God's Word.

Over the years, there are familiar scriptures that I return to over and over. But at different times in my life, I may receive a different message from a scripture passage that I have read many times before. This tells me that, like God, His Word is alive and relevant to me today.

After I received the gift of the Holy Spirit, I was given a reading assignment. God spoke one word to me, and it was the word *Proverbs*. Once I began to read Proverbs, I felt it was a very fitting first assignment. Proverbs 1:1-7 (NIV 1984) states:

The proverbs of Solomon, son of David, king of Israel: for attaining wisdom and discipline; for understanding words of insight; for acquiring a disciplined and prudent life, doing what is right and just and fair; or giving prudence to the simple, knowledge and discretion to the young— let the wise listen and add to their learning, and let the discerning get guidance— for understanding proverbs and parables, the sayings and riddles of the wise.

The fear of the LORD is the beginning of knowledge, but fools despise wisdom and discipline.

This was a good starting place for me. Proverbs gave me a better understanding of God's expectations of me and instructions on living a godly life.

Prayer

As I stated earlier, prayer is nothing more than you talking to God and listening for God's response. Many people have the misconception that prayer should be very formal and regimented. God knows who you are, so come to Him in your own way. You cannot hide anything from God, so you might as well be honest as well. So, that begs the question, "If God knows everything, why do I have to pray?"

We should pray because Jesus, the Son of God, felt it necessary to pray. Not only did Jesus pray but he taught his disciples to pray as well. In Matthew 6:9-13 (NIV), Jesus says:

Learning about God

> This, then, is how you should pray: "Our Father in heaven, hallowed be your name, your kingdom come, your will be done on earth as it is in heaven. Give us today our daily bread. Forgive us our debts, as we also have forgiven our debtors. And lead us not into temptation but deliver us from the evil one."

This passage is commonly referred to as the Lord's Prayer. What can we learn from this prayer? The prayer begins with an acknowledgment of who God is and praise to God—"Our Father in heaven, hallowed be your name." Then the prayer acknowledges God's power and authority in heaven but also requests that the same power and authority be released on earth—"Your kingdom come, your will be done on earth as it is in heaven." "Give us today our daily bread," is a reminder that God can and will supply our daily needs. The prayer includes a request for forgiveness of sins—"forgive us our debts." But we are also reminded to forgive others—"as we also have forgiven our debtors." And finally, the prayer closes with a request to help us stay on the narrow path that leads to righteousness and protect us from evil—"and lead us not into temptation, but deliver us from the evil one." Based on Jesus' words, it is not a question of whether we should pray. Jesus expects us to pray and this is how we should do it. Jesus has given us a blueprint for prayer:

1) Acknowledge who God is to you.
2) Praise God. Worship Him. This will be different for everyone. But most importantly, your praise and worship should be genuine and sincere.

3) Acknowledge God's authority and surrender your will for God's will.
4) Express your cares, concerns, and worries. Thank God for meeting the needs you have today. You can also thank God for meeting the needs of others.
5) Confess your sins and ask for forgiveness. Remember to forgive others for their wrongs. The amount of forgiveness you extend to others is the amount of forgiveness God will extend to you (Matthew 6:14-15, Colossians 3:13).
6) Ask that you are not tempted by things that will lead you away from God. And finally, ask for protection from evil.

What better example do we need than the example that Jesus set for us? I was taught that we should end our prayers with a statement such as "in Jesus' name I pray" or "in the name of Jesus I pray." The idea behind ending your prayer this way is that Jesus is the Advocate who petitions God on your behalf. The statement is like the stamp that is needed to get a letter to its destination. But Romans 8:26-27 (NLT) tells us of another that advocates for us also, the Holy Spirit. "And the Holy Spirit helps us in our weakness. For example, we don't know what God wants us to pray for. But the Holy Spirit prays for us with groanings that cannot be expressed in words. And the Father who knows all hearts knows what the Spirit is saying, for the Spirit pleads for us believers in harmony with God's own will." So, even when we don't know what to pray or how to pray, God's Spirit intervenes for us according to God's will which is perfect.

Another important reason to pray is to build a foundation of trust in your relationship with God. Trust is an important part of any relationship, but it is not an instantaneous thing.

It is built over time as you interact with each other. Trust involves recognizing the other person's needs and ensuring those needs are met. When I think about trust, I think about the relationship between a mother and her newborn baby. When the baby cries, the mother tries to figure out what the problem is and fix it. Over time, the baby learns to trust that when she cries, she gets noticed and the problem gets addressed. And the mother learns the difference between a cry for hunger and a cry for a soiled diaper. This cycle of expressing a problem and fulfilling the need builds trust and love between the mother and her baby. The same is true in our relationship with God. In the *New Living Translation*, Psalm 23 speaks of the trust we should have in God.

> The Lord is my shepherd; I have all I need.
>
> He lets me rest in green meadows; he leads me beside peaceful streams.
>
> He renews my strength. He guides me along right paths, bringing honor to his name.
>
> Even when I walk through the darkest valley, I will not be afraid, for you are close beside me. Your rod and your staff protect and comfort me.
>
> You prepare a feast for me in the presence of my enemies. You honor me by anointing my head with oil. My cup overflows with blessings.
>
> Surely your goodness and unfailing love will pursue me all the days of my life, and I will live in the house of the Lord forever.

Salvation

In this Psalm, David expresses complete confidence in God's ability to provide for our needs, guide and protect us, and bless us abundantly even in the midst of danger. But it is not just about you trusting God, it is also about God trusting you.

Another key reason to pray is that prayer activates the possibilities that God has for you. In Matthew 19:26 (NIV), Jesus tells us, "But with God all things are possible." The word *with* implies a partnership between you and God. But to access the power of that partnership, you must be in relationship with God. Part of the way we solidify that relationship is through prayer. So, when we pray, we must earnestly believe that God can answer our prayers. That doesn't mean the answer to every prayer will be yes. God may not answer the prayer the way we think it should be answered. But this is why trust is such an important part of the relationship. We must understand that whatever the answer may be, God has our best interest in mind.

Prayer is also an important tool to help us deal with the stresses and strains of life. Philippians 4:6-7 (NIV) states, "Do not be anxious about anything, but in every situation, by prayer and petition, with thanksgiving, present your requests to God. And the peace of God, which transcends all understanding, will guard your hearts and your minds in Christ Jesus." We often carry around needless burdens when we could easily turn our problems over to God. I bring my struggles to God, and He helps me work through them. Prayer is not just about waiting until you have some big problem in your life and then running to God for help. Prayer should be an ongoing dialogue between you and God every day.

To get the most out of your prayer life, you need to set aside dedicated time for prayer that is free from distractions.

Learning about God

In other words, that means no television, no music, no radio, and no cell phone. Just you and God. God can hear you through anything. But *we* need that quietness to hear God. Most of the time, God speaks to us in whispers. He also speaks to us through scripture. To hear God, our spirit needs to listen and be still. Ultimately, we have a choice to listen to God or not listen to Him. If we are distracted by noise and chaos, we may not hear the whispers.

Don't get me wrong, I pray to God all the time—at work, in the car, and even standing in line at the grocery store. But when I really need to connect with God, it's me in a quiet place with my Bible or a scripture-based devotional. I begin each session by reading scripture or a devotional. Then I begin my discussion with God. I thank Him for the opportunity to see a new day and the many blessings He has bestowed upon me. I ask forgiveness for my sins. I pray for others in need of prayer, and I pray for my family and friends. Finally, I pray for myself.

I invite the Holy Spirit and ask God to use me as He sees fit. I ask God for the ability to love others as He loves us. And then I wait. Sometimes I get an answer immediately. Sometimes I may not get an answer for days or even weeks. Sometimes my answer is a scripture. But I know that I can always bring my petitions to God openly and honestly with no holds barred. In 1 John 5:14-15 (NIV), we are reminded that we can be confident as we approach God when we are in His will, and it states, "This is the confidence we have in approaching God: that if we ask anything according to his will, he hears us. And if we know that he hears us—whatever we ask—we know that we have what we asked of him."

I have found there is no better way for me to start my day than in prayer. But life being life, I don't always have the time to spend thirty or forty minutes in prayer every day. Being a wife, a mother, and a physician means life can be hectic. Sometimes my day begins with, "We need you at the hospital now" or I had a sick child at the bedroom door. In that case, I thank God for another day and quickly ask for His guidance for me.

More than anything, God wants your relationship with Him to be personal. What works for me may not work for you. I have included my ritual as an example. You must decide what works best for you. Start slowly. Set aside ten or fifteen minutes a day for prayer. If that's too much, start with five minutes a day. Once you make prayer a part of your daily routine, you will find you want to spend more and more time in prayer.

The Holy Spirit

Inviting the Holy Spirit to live within you is an essential part of the Christian journey. Once we have opened our hearts to God and turned away from our sinful nature, we have the opportunity to receive the gift of the Holy Spirit. This miraculous gift from God has served a multitude of functions since the beginning of time. It was the Spirit of God that hovered over the waters when the world was formed (Genesis 1:2). This amazing gift from God is an Advocate (John 14:16; 15:26), Counselor, Teacher (John 14:26; 1 John 2:27), Guide (John 16:13), Intercessor (Romans 8:26–27), Revealer of Truth (John 14:17), Spirit of Life (Romans 8:11), Witness (Romans 8:16, Hebrews 8:15), Seal (2 Corinthians 1:22, 5:5; Ephesians 1:13-14), and Convicter of Sin (John 16:7-11). God's Spirit provides everything we need to repent of our sins, serve God, and lead us on the path to eternal life. We cannot make it in this world as believers without the Holy Spirit.

The Holy Spirit is an empowering Spirit who is meant to give us the strength and courage to face the challenges of life. It is through the power of the Holy Spirit that we can put sin to death and affirm the Spirit of Life that will bring us into eternity with our Lord and Savior, Jesus Christ. It is the deposit or seal of the Holy Spirit that Christ will be looking for upon His return. When you belong to God, He gives you a portion of Himself as a gift. And that gift is the Holy Spirit. In conjunction with prayer, it is the Holy Spirit that keeps us connected to God. As mentioned previously, it is the Holy Spirit who is our conscience, our moral compass, and our ever-present connection to God.

I would, however, guess that the presence of the Holy Spirit is what most people are missing in their relationship with God. I believe it is missing in the person who calls himself or herself a Christian but doesn't hesitate to spew hatred and perpetuate prejudice, injustice, and evil.

Inviting the Holy Spirit to dwell within us is also probably the most difficult aspect of our relationship with God because it requires us to remove all the barriers between us and God. We must be willing to relinquish authority over our lives to God. For a long time, I was unwilling to do this, and it hindered my relationship with God. I was going to church. I was reading my Bible, but I could never understand how to make my relationship with God personal. The barrier to me receiving the Holy Spirit was pride. As a doctor, I felt I could not commit myself wholeheartedly to something I couldn't prove or see. I was worried about what my colleagues or other people would think of me if I expressed my love for God openly and without reservations. It was only after I was willing to remove that barrier that I was able to fully cultivate a meaningful relationship with God. Now, I don't care what other people think about my relationship with God. The benefits of my relationship with God far outweigh the perceptions of people who don't know Him.

Most people come to God when chaos or turmoil disrupts their life. I am no exception. The thing that finally allowed me to remove the barrier between me and God was the accident involving my son. His accident helped me move from the confession that I had made with my mouth to believing in God and opening my whole heart to Him. When I finally decided that my pride was in the way, and I was willing to let go of it, that is when I was finally saved. Almost immediately, there was a dramatic change in my outlook on life. Don't get me wrong—I still had a lot of growing to do as a Christian. But removing the barrier of pride was an important step in my journey with God.

Search your soul and find out what it is that is separating you from a full relationship with God. Is it greed, lust, or concern about lacking something or missing out on something? Until that barrier is removed and you are willing to relinquish all authority over your life to God, you cannot achieve the fullness of the relationship God desires to have with you. Don't think of it so much as what you must give up, instead, think of what you will gain. You can gain the fruit of the Spirit as described in Galatians 5:22 (NIV), which is "love, joy, peace, forbearance, kindness, goodness, faithfulness, gentleness and self-control." These gifts cannot be bought at any price but are given freely by God. Who among us doesn't want more love, peace, and joy in our lives? And I can always use more self-control, kindness, goodness, gentleness, and faithfulness. There is no need to be concerned about lacking something. God, the Creator of the universe, has everything you could ever want or need.

Learning about God

To grow and move forward on the salvation journey you must learn more about God for yourself. A fulfilling relationship requires intimacy that can only be obtained by spending time with each other and learning more about each other. Read your Bible, pray, and allow the Holy Spirit to lead and guide you.

NOTES

Chapter 3

WHAT KIND OF RELATIONSHIP DO YOU WANT TO HAVE WITH GOD?

I think it's amazing that the Creator of the universe wants to be in relationship with each and every one of us. From the time Adam and Eve were kicked out of the Garden of Eden, God has been trying to re-establish the relationship with humanity. He made a covenant with the people of Israel to be their God, and they would be His people. Leviticus 26:12 (NKJV) tells us, "I will walk among you and be your God, and you shall be My people." And when our sins separated us from Him again, God gave His son, Jesus Christ, who was willing to die on the cross for us (John 3:16). All this was done so God could remain in relationship with humanity. I know God desires a relationship with us. The question becomes, what kind of relationship do you want to have with God?

Before we talk about what kind of relationship we want to have with God, I think it's important we discuss why we should be in relationship with God at all. As the Creator of the universe, God *designed* us to be in relationship with him. We are made in God's image. Genesis 1:26 (NIV) says, "Then God said, 'Let us make mankind in our image, in our likeness,'" and Genesis 2:7 (NIV) describes our creation

"Then the Lord God formed a man from the dust of the ground and breathed into his nostrils the breath of life, and the man became a living being." Not only did God make us in his image but God put a part of Himself into us when He created us. That part of God within us desires to reconnect with God. The God within us desires to worship Him and be in relationship with Him. Until the Spirit of God within us reconnects with God, we are prone to feeling empty, hollow, lost, and alone. Many of us try to fill this emptiness with poor substitutes for the Spirit of God. For some, it's alcohol, money, drugs, sex, power, or bad relationships with human beings. But none of those things can make us feel whole like the Spirit of God can.

It is a relationship with God that allows us to feel whole and helps us fulfill our purpose in life. I know some of you are thinking, "I can have a fulfilling life if I am not in relationship with God." There are millions of people walking around on this earth with what they consider fulfilling lives, who are not in relationship with God. But I believe they are missing out on so much. I like to think of it as the difference between sirloin steak and filet mignon. Yes, sirloin steak is good. And if you've never had filet mignon, you are probably going to be happy with the sirloin. But filet mignon is oh so much better. And once you've tasted it, you probably won't want to settle for the sirloin anymore. So, do you want a good relationship with God, or do you want the best possible relationship with God?

Many of us would like a better relationship with God but are not willing to invest the time or the energy that requires. For many of us, our relationship with God consists of calling on God when we are in crisis and then not thinking about God again until another crisis arises. Or we think about God on Sunday while we are in church, and don't think about Him again until the next time we are back in church. A relationship with God can be so much more fulfilling than that. Imagine having a relationship with someone that you can talk to anytime, anywhere, twenty-four hours a day, seven days a week. A relationship with God is one in which you are loved unconditionally and forgiven an unlimited number of times when you make mistakes. Imagine a relationship that can provide comfort when you are stressed, provide healing when you are sick, and peace in the middle of turmoil. Imagine a relationship that can improve your relationship with your family and friends and make you a better spouse, sibling, or parent. Why wouldn't you want a relationship like that with God? Because it requires more than most of us are willing to give. It means putting God first and others ahead of ourselves. It can be the most fulfilling and rewarding relationship of your life if you choose to pursue it.

When I think of the things that prevented me from having a more fulfilling relationship with God, it came down to personal choices. Initially, I was not aware that my pride prevented me from having a more fulfilling relationship with God. Once I was willing to relinquish my pride, my relationship with God changed instantly. Not only did my relationship with God change, but I was also changed—and people noticed. I heard from friends and coworkers that something about me was different. I felt like my improved relationship with God made me a better wife, a better mother, a better physician, and a better friend. Once I overcame the hurdle of pride, then time became my biggest obstacle. Being a wife, a mother, and a physician means I am busy. If I'm being totally honest, sometimes my prayer life and devotional time got neglected. I became one of those people who sought God in

Salvation

a crisis. When things were going well in my life, I neglected God until another crisis arose. But I was missing out on so much when I limited my relationship with God like that.

So, ask yourself—what kind of relationship do I want with God? How much time and energy am I willing to invest in the relationship? What are the obstacles that are preventing me from having a better relationship with God? Answer these questions, and you've already taken another step on your salvation journey.

NOTES

Chapter 4

THE BENEFITS OF A LIVING FAITH

No conversation about salvation would be complete without a discussion about faith. In times of adversity, I've often heard people say, "You've just got to have faith." If you haven't been exposed to the teachings of Jesus Christ, the concept of faith may not be familiar to you. Or you may have some idea of what faith means but don't really understand the role of faith in your relationship with God. What part does faith play in the salvation journey? It is essential to our relationship with God. Therefore, it's important that we understand the importance of faith on our journey. Although it seems like such a little word, faith is a huge part of our salvation journey. We use the word faith all the time, but have you ever considered what it takes to have the faith we so often speak of? There are building blocks that make our faith real. The building blocks of faith are belief, hope, trust, confidence, patience, and endurance.

Faith begins with belief. It is that belief that allows us to establish a relationship with God through His Son, Jesus Christ. Hebrews 11:6 (NIV) tells us of the importance of faith, "And without faith it is impossible to please God, because anyone who comes to him must believe that he exists and that he rewards those who earnestly seek him." Let's look at it this way. How good is your relationship with someone if you don't trust them, don't believe the things they tell you, and don't believe the promises they make to you? It's no different with God. We must believe God is who He says He is, and we must believe that God keeps His promises. It is by faith that we believe in the saving works of Jesus Christ. But it is by the grace of God that we have access to the gift of salvation.

Another essential element of faith is hope. Hope is the desire for something to happen and the belief that it can happen or be true. Hebrews 11:1 (NIV) says, "Now faith is confidence in what we hope for and assurance about what we do not see." If we have no hope, we have no faith. Hope allows us to believe that all things are possible and keeps us going from day to day. It is the desire to see this broken world one day restored to its full glory and wholeness by God. If we have a bad day, hope allows us to believe we will have a better day tomorrow.

In addition to belief and hope, faith requires trust. Proverbs 3:5 (NIV) says, "Trust in the Lord with all your heart and lean not on your own understanding." Trust requires us to follow God's directives even when we don't understand God's will. Trusting God means knowing God wants what's best for you. Trust is something that develops over time during the course of a relationship. Faith allows us to trust God and believe that what God promises is true. The more experiences you have with God, the more you will learn to trust Him.

To have faith, we must also have confidence. But this is not confidence in ourselves but in the work of Jesus Christ. Hebrews 10:19-22 (NIV) reveals, "Therefore, brothers and sisters, since we have confidence to enter the Most Holy Place by the blood of Jesus ... and since we have a great priest over the house of God, let us draw near to God with a sincere heart and with the full assurance that faith brings." The confidence that Jesus conquered sin through His work on the cross is what gives our faith meaning. Because of Jesus' death and resurrection, we can have confidence in our relationship with God. We can confidently come to God through our relationship with Jesus Christ and know that God sees us through the perfection of Jesus Christ and not our sin. We can be confident of God's love for us. And we can also be confident in His grace and mercy towards us.

Faith also requires patience and endurance. The salvation journey is not always easy. We need to understand that the Holy Spirit is constantly working on our behalf. But we also need to understand that God works in His time, not ours. Psalm 27:14 (NLT) says, "Wait patiently for the Lord. Be brave and courageous. Yes, wait patiently for the Lord." So, we must wait patiently on God. Be patient with the expectation that God has heard your cries. And at the right time, He will intervene in your situation. While we wait, we are to pray, praise God, and worship Him. But in addition to patience, faith needs endurance. This journey is a marathon, not a sprint. James 1:3-4 (NIV) reminds us, "Because you know that the testing of your faith produces perseverance. Let perseverance finish its work so that you may be mature and complete, not lacking anything." I've heard it said that a faith that is not tested is not faith. It is through our trials that our faith is strengthened and grows.

Now that we have an understanding of the building blocks of faith, we can continue our discussion about faith, but not just any kind of faith—a living faith. Let's explore what I mean by a living faith. A living faith is rooted in hope, tested and strengthened by life's experiences, and affirmed by the Word of God. A living faith—the kind of faith that pleases God—incorporates faithfulness to God, absolute trust in God, and confident assurance that God will keep His promises. It seems the world we live in is getting crazier and more chaotic by the day. In today's world, a living faith is needed. We have seen a world overtaken by a pandemic and death, and plagued with hatred, violence, corruption, and injustice. We are certainly living in perilous times. It's times like these that it's easy to become hopeless and feel disenfranchised. But that's not what we need in perilous times.

It is times like these that require a living faith. This is not the kind of faith you pick up on Sunday morning and put down on Sunday afternoon. I'm talking about a living, breathing faith. It's this kind of faith that gets you out of bed in the morning when all you want to do is pull the covers up over your head. This kind of faith lets us press on through the storms of life with the confident hope that something better is waiting on the other side. A living faith stands up to oppression, hatred, and violence and challenges injustice. A living faith seeks the truth. This is the kind of faith that Hebrews 11:6 describes. This kind of faith is essential to our relationship with God.

We talk about faith all the time, but faith is a word that can have many meanings. It can refer to faithfulness—like the good and faithful servant found in Matthew 24:45, who looks after the master's household and feeds the other servants while the master is gone. Faith can mean absolute trust such as the story in Luke 7:2-10 about the centurion with a sick servant who sent word, asking Jesus to come and heal his servant. But before Jesus could make His way to the centurion's house, the centurion sent his friends to tell Jesus, "Lord, don't trouble yourself, for I do not deserve to have you come under my roof. ... But say the word, and my servant will be healed" (Luke 7:6-7 NIV). When Jesus heard this, He was amazed and told the crowd following Him, "I tell you, I have not found such great faith even in Israel" (Luke 7:9 NIV).[1]

Faith can also mean the confident hope we find in Hebrews 11:1 (NIV), "Now faith is confidence in what we hope for and assurance about what we do not see." But faith can also be a barren belief as described in James 2:14-26. A dead faith knows and believes the gospel of Jesus Christ, but those beliefs fail to change the heart or one's behavior. In other words, there should be evidence of your faith in the way you live and your actions; when that doesn't happen, your faith is dead.[2]

We need to understand that faith is a gift from God. Ephesians 2:8 (NIV) tells us, "For it is by grace you have been saved, through faith—and this is not from yourselves, it is the gift of God." Here, Paul ties faith closely to salvation. It is because of God's infinite mercy that He gives us faith when He saves us. We can never come to God through our own faith because our faith would never be good enough for God. Instead, we must accept God's offer of faith and allow Him to plant the seed of faith within us. Yes, faith is a seed. Jesus tells us in Matthew 17:20 (NIV) that we only need a little. "If you have faith as small as a mustard seed." But, oh, what amazing things can happen when we feed that seed of faith with the Word of God, nurture that seed with prayer, shine the light of the Holy Spirit on that seed, and encourage it to grow by trusting God. It is then that it becomes a living faith—a faith that is able to withstand the struggles of life and the fiery darts of the enemy.

A living faith is a call to action. However, no amount of good work can make up for a lack of faith. But as James tells us in 2:26 (KJV), "faith without works is dead." The way we live our lives and the things that we do for God and others should be evidence of our faith. If our faith does not produce a change in our hearts *and* good works, then our faith is dead. James also tells us in verses 21 and 22 (NIV) "Was not our ancestor Abraham considered righteous for what he did when he offered his son Isaac on the altar? You see that his faith and his actions were working together, and his faith was made complete by what he did." The point that James is making here is that faith and action should go hand and hand. Your faith should drive your actions, and it is through your actions and good works that your faith grows.

It is when we put our faith into action that we please God. It is our faith and love of God that call us to act. Let's look at Philippians 4:9 (NIV), "Whatever you have learned or received or heard from me or seen in me—put it into practice." Paul is telling us to put the things that we have learned about God and from God into practice, and the God of peace will be with us. We cannot allow hatred, injustice, and oppression to thrive. We cannot allow poverty and hunger to flourish. A living faith requires us to act. God expects us to act. It is your actions that make your faith alive and complete.

It is when we put our faith into action that God activates His power within us. It is faith that opens the door to possibility. Mark 10:27 (NIV) tells us, "All things are possible with God." But for things to be possible, we must first believe in the possibility. Believing in the possibility is the essence of faith. It allows us to enter the realm of the impossible. It is faith—a living, breathing faith—that allows us to see a faithful, loving God with unlimited resources and not our seemingly impossible situation.

I think about the many times God has blessed me with exactly what I needed exactly when I needed it. One of those times was shortly after I started my own practice. The practice had been open for about six months, and up to that point, I was not taking a paycheck. I was using loans and what little income the practice was generating to pay the bills and pay the staff. That particular Saturday, my husband was preparing to pay our household bills. Our personal savings were depleted, and the little bit of money in our checking account was not going to cover our household expenses. He pleaded with me to pay myself something, even if it was only $500. So, I headed over to the office to go over the books and see if I could find enough money to pay myself. After going over the books at the office, I realized I did not have enough money to pay myself the amount my husband requested. When I got home that afternoon, I picked up the mail on my way into the house. In the mail was an unexpected check for $5,000—ten times the amount my husband requested. God proved to me that day He could and would supply my needs, turning what seemed like an impossible situation into the possible.

It is when we believe in the possibility of the impossible that our faith comes to life. There are numerous benefits to a living faith. I would like to focus on three of the benefits a living faith provides. A living faith provides protection, provides peace, and sustains us. Let's look at how a living faith provides protection. Hebrews Chapter 11 shows us what faith can do for us and gives us examples of men and women of faith. I like to think of it as the faith hall of fame. Noah is one of those examples. Noah was a righteous man living in a corrupt world. God warned Noah that He was going to destroy the world in a flood. Prior to that time, there had never been a flood or even rain. In faith, Noah believed God and built an ark. Noah's faith was rewarded, and he and his family were saved from the flood when the rest of the world was destroyed.

Another example of God's protection is found in the story of the parting of the Red Sea. By faith, the children of Israel were able to walk through the Red Sea on dry land, but Pharaoh's army was destroyed (Exodus 14:22-23). And, just as Moses believed in God's ability to provide protection, it is through faith that we can believe Isaiah 54:17 (NLT) which says, "But in that coming day no weapon turned against you will succeed. You will silence every voice raised up to accuse you. These benefits are enjoyed by the servants of the Lord." This scripture speaks of the protection God affords to those who believe in Him. Even though people will try to attack you, those attacks will not be successful. This doesn't mean that the attack or the accusation isn't going to happen; it means that it will not lead to destruction.

We must believe that God is willing and able to protect us. It is hope that gives us the faith to believe. Psalm 18:2 (NLT) reminds us, "The Lord is my rock, my fortress, and my savior; my God is my rock, in whom I find protection. He is my shield, the power that saves me, and my place of safety." And Psalm 91:14 (NLT) tells us, "The Lord says, 'I will rescue those who love me. I will protect those who trust in my name.'" Faith in God provides protection in a corrupt and evil world. I would not want to exist in today's world without faith in God. It is my faith in God that protects me from the dangers of the world we live in. It is my faith in God that has protected me from the enemy's attacks.

The second benefit of living faith is peace. Yes, our world is in chaos, but a living faith allows us to find peace in the middle of chaos. That peace is found in Jesus Christ. In John 14:27 (NIV), Jesus tells us, "Peace I leave with you; my peace I give you. I do not give to you as the world gives. Do not let your hearts be troubled and do not be afraid." Jesus has given us His peace. He has left it here for us whenever we need it. That peace is found through prayer and thanksgiving.

Philippians 4: 6-7 (NIV) states, "Do not be anxious about anything, but in every situation, by prayer and petition, with thanksgiving, present your requests to God. And the peace of God, which transcends all understanding, will guard your hearts and your minds in Christ Jesus." You see, it is Jesus who provides peace, and it is Jesus who guards your heart and your mind against the chaos around you. But this is not just any kind of peace; this is supernatural peace. This is a peace that allows you to find rest and comfort in the middle of chaos. So, when you find yourself in turmoil, focus on Jesus, and His peace will find you.

I think about the many hospitalizations, surgeries, and procedures that my son Jayden has been through, and how many life-threatening situations he has survived. Jesus' peace has always been there. Sometimes I have had to go looking for it, but as my faith has grown, Jesus' peace has found me in the middle of chaotic situations.

Another benefit of a living faith is that it is sustaining. It is in perilous times that our faith is more important than ever. A living faith carries us from day to day because we know we can trust God and not worry about our present situation. A living faith allows us to endure trials, mistreatment, and abuse from the world because we know God has something better for us in eternity. When I think about what African Americans as a people have endured, I know it was faith that brought us to the present day, and faith that will carry us into the future. In the words of the Negro National Anthem:

> God of our weary years, God of our silent tears,
> Thou who has brought us thus far on the way,
> Thou who has by Thy might led us into the light
> Keep us forever in the path, we pray.[3]

A living faith gives us the courage to face the giants in life because we know we never have to face anything alone. We can trust and believe what Deuteronomy 31:8 (NIV) tells us, "The Lord himself goes before you and will be with you; he will never leave you nor forsake you. Do not be afraid; do not be discouraged." God goes before you and will be with you in every situation you face. A living faith believes Philippians 4:19 (NIV), "And my God will meet all your needs according to the riches of his glory in Christ Jesus." Not only will God be with you, but He will provide for you every step along the way.

It is through faith that we can persevere, even when God's promises are not immediately fulfilled. When we look at the men and women in the faith hall of fame in Hebrews Chapter 11, none of them saw God's promise themselves. The promises that God made were not *for* them, but it was *through* these people that God's promises were fulfilled. The *Message Bible* puts it this way, "Not one of these people, even though their lives of faith were exemplary, got their hands on what was promised. God had a better plan for us: that their faith and our faith would come together to make one completed whole, their lives of faith not complete apart from ours." (Hebrews 11:39-40, MSG). This passage tells us that sometimes our faith must be combined with the faith of others to bring God's promises to pass. So, when it seems like God's promises are not coming to fruition, understand that God has a better plan—a bigger picture than you can see or understand. Even though we sometimes find ourselves waiting on God, it is in faith that we can wait patiently for God to fulfill His promises. And when you wonder if God is worth waiting on, understand He has something much better than you could ever imagine. Ephesians 3:20 (NKJV) tells us, "Now to Him who is able to do exceedingly abundantly above all that we ask or think, according to the power that works in us."

It is through life's struggles that our faith is tested and strengthened. Paul reminds us in 2 Corinthians 4:8-9 (NKJV), "*We are* hard pressed on every side, yet not crushed; *we are* perplexed, but not in despair; persecuted, but not forsaken; struck down, but not destroyed." It is because of faith that we are not crushed. It is because of faith that we are not in despair and we are not forsaken. It is because of faith that we are not destroyed. It is a living faith that protects us and gives us peace in the middle of troubling times. It is a living faith that sustains us from day to day. With the chaos in the world today, now is not the time to be caught with a dead faith. We need to believe in God and not in what we see going on around us. We need to trust that God will keep His promises. But we also need to be obedient to God.

A living faith believes that God exists, acts on that belief, and is rewarded for the belief and the actions. On your salvation journey, you will be called to use your faith over and over. A living faith is essential for survival in perilous times and invaluable on the salvation journey. A living faith is necessary to please God.

I have some questions for you about faith. Do you have faith? If so, what have you done with the gift of faith that God has given you? Has your faith grown since you received it from God? Do you treat your faith like a pretty crystal vase and put it on the shelf? Or, do you actually use it? Have you prayed for God to increase your faith? Do you treat your faith like your cell phone and carry it wherever you go? What have you done with your faith?

NOTES

Chapter 5

How to Love Like God

As human beings, we want to love, and we want to be loved. This is a basic need for us. God designed us to love and to be loved, and He commands us over and over to love one another. We all have ideas of what love is. There's romantic love, brotherly love, family love, and even self-love. But so often our understanding of love is flawed. We think of love as a feeling and often describe love in terms of "falling in love," which describes a love that we have no control over. Or we use terms such as "I love those shoes" or "I love my new car," which diminishes the value of the word love.

The type of love that God gives to us is about action. God's love is a purposeful act, and the kind of love that God expects from us requires us to purposefully put the needs of others before our own needs. We know of love because God has shown us what love is. And He wants us to love as He loves. First John 3:16 (NIV) says, "This is how we know what love is: Jesus Christ laid down his life for us. And we ought to lay down our lives for our brothers and sisters." God's love is all-encompassing, all-inclusive, and unrestricted. God loves us freely and wants us to love each other the same way. First John 4:7 (NIV) tells us, "Dear friends, let us love one another, for love comes from God. Everyone who loves has been born of God and knows God."

To love like God, we need to have a better understanding of God's love, which is an unconditional, eternal, and perfect love that we know as *agape love*. God loves us no matter what. God's unconditional love is rooted in forgiveness and filled with mercy and grace. It is a love that can look past our transgressions and see our needs. God's unconditional love is the greatest example we can follow. Paul speaks of this in Romans 8: 38-39 (NIV), "For I am convinced that neither death nor life, neither angels nor demons, neither the present nor the future, nor any powers, neither height nor depth, nor anything else in all creation, will be able to separate us from the love of God that is in Christ Jesus our Lord." Nothing can separate us from God's love. This is a powerful reality.

One of the tricks of the enemy is to convince you that you don't deserve God's love, or you're not good enough for God to love you, or you've done something so bad that God can never forgive you. Nothing could be further from the truth. God loves you just as you are. In actuality, none of us will ever be good enough for God's love. Romans 3:23 (NKJV) tells us, "For all have sinned and fall short of the glory of God." That's where God's grace and mercy come in. And that's why God sent His Son Jesus to cover our shortcomings. Psalm 103:8-11 (NLT) speaks to God's compassion and love for us. "The Lord is compassionate and merciful, slow to get angry and filled with unfailing love. He will not constantly accuse us, nor remain angry forever. He does not punish us for all our sins; he does not deal harshly with us, as we deserve. For his unfailing love toward those who fear him is as great as the height of the heavens above the earth." God does not expect us to be perfect. In fact, in His infinite mercy, God is willing to forgive us over and over when we make mistakes.

God's love is an eternal love. God's love was manifest at the beginning of creation and will exist forever. First Corinthians 13 tells us that prophecies will cease, tongues will be stilled, and knowledge will pass away, but love will remain. Love will never fail. I'm so glad I serve a God who will love me forever! Isn't it wonderful that God's love is forever? Isaiah 54:10 (NIV) also tells us of God's eternal love, "'Though the mountains be shaken, and the hills be removed, yet my unfailing love for you will not be shaken nor my covenant of peace be removed,' says the Lord who has compassion on you.'" The things of this world will not last forever, but God's love will last forever.

We must know God to understand the magnitude of His love. We come to know God through our experiences with Him, spending time in prayer, and studying His Word. Like Paul told the church in Ephesus, once you know who God is, then you can begin to "grasp how wide and long and high and deep is the love of Christ, and to know this love that surpasses knowledge—that you may be filled to the measure of all the fullness of God" (Ephesians 3:18-19, NIV). Once you know God, then you can understand what love is. But it is not enough to know God. Once we know Him, He expects us to become more like Him and love as He loves.

In addition to being eternal and unconditional, God's love is perfect. Despite our shortcomings, imperfections, and sinfulness God loves us. God knows us fully with all our faults and weaknesses and yet loves us fully with all our faults and imperfections. God knows everything we've ever done and loves us anyway. First Corinthians

13:4-7, 13 (NIV) tells us what perfect love looks like: Love is patient, love is kind. It does not envy, it does not boast, it is not proud. It is not rude, it is not self-seeking, it is not easily angered, it keeps no record of wrongs. Love does not delight in evil but rejoices with the truth. It always protects, always trusts, always hopes, always perseveres. Love never fails . . . And now these three remain: faith, hope and love. But the greatest of these is love.

God is patient and compassionate with us. Despite our repeated disobedience and rejection of Him, He is slow to anger and throws our transgressions into the sea of forgetfulness when we earnestly repent. He forgives us. He watches over us and protects us. He loves us perfectly, even though we are imperfect.

Once we understand the nature of God's love, then we can begin to love like God. In Mark 12:30-31 (NKJV), Jesus says, "'And you shall love the LORD your God with all your heart, with all your soul, with all your mind, and with all your strength.' This is the first commandment. And the second, like it, is this: 'You shall love your neighbor as yourself.' There is no other commandment greater than these.'" And again, in John 13:34 (NIV), Jesus says, "A new command I give you: Love one another. As I have loved you, so you must love one another."

Yes, God wants us to love Him, but He also wants us to love each other as He loves us. It is easy to love those who love you. But what about the people who don't love you or the people who don't even like you? Are we supposed to love them too? Yes! God still expects us to love them. In Luke 6:27-28 (NIV), Jesus reminds us that we are to love our enemies. "But to you who are listening I say: Love your enemies, do good to those who hate you, bless those who curse you, pray for those who mistreat you." And in

Luke 6:32-33(NIV) Jesus says, "If you love those who love you, what credit is that to you? Even sinners love those who love them. And if you do good to those who are good to you, what credit is that to you? Even sinners do that."

God expects us to love everyone. When you love your enemy and do good things for them, eventually the hate in their heart is replaced with love. Proverbs 25:21-22 (NIV) tells us, "If your enemy is hungry, give him food to eat; if he is thirsty, give him water to drink. In doing this, you will heap burning coals on his head, and the Lord will reward you." It is love that breaks down barriers. It is love that opens doors. It is love that changes people. Love that will win in the end. The Roman poet Virgil understood this when he wrote *"Amor Vincit Omnia,"* which means "love conquers all things."

To love like God, we must look past our differences and see the humanity in each other. To love like God, we must embrace our differences in race, ethnicity, gender, religious affiliation, and sexual orientation. To love like God, we must be filled with his Spirit. When we are filled with God's Spirit, that is when we can look past each other's faults and see each other's needs, we can forgive each other's transgressions, and we can love our enemies. It is the presence of God's Spirit that allows us to care for others more than we care about ourselves. In the end, we are all human beings no matter what color we are, no matter our gender, and no matter whom we love. And God commands us to love one another. This is a commandment, not a suggestion. Jesus showed us the greatest example of love the world has ever seen when He died on the cross for us. As the Son of God, Jesus, the one who knew no sin, took on the sins of the whole world. That is love like no other love. God loved the world so much that He gave His best for us. John 3:16 (NIV) tells us, "For God so loved the world, that he gave his one and only Son, that whoever believes in him shall not perish but have eternal life."

Loving like God is the ultimate outward expression of your relationship with Him. Being able to love as God loves requires you to be in relationship with God and to be filled with His Holy Spirit. And when you are filled with God's love, you'll want to love others as God loves you.

NOTES

Chapter 6

God's Love in Action

When you truly love God and are in a relationship with Him, your life will be a reflection of the Spirit of God that is within you. God's goal is for you to learn about Him, become more like Him, and share what you've learned about God with others. When something is this good, why keep it to yourself? There are different ways to share your love of God with others. We have all been given different gifts that are to be used to spread God's love and build His kingdom. Ultimately, God is love, and we are to be an expression of God's love on earth.

Loving God is a wonderful thing, but the relationship should not stop there. Our first responsibility is to love God with all our heart. Our second responsibility is to love our brothers and sisters. We cannot claim to love God but then mistreat our fellow brothers and sisters. First John 4:20-21 (NKJV) reminds us, "If someone says, 'I love God,' and hates his brother, he is a liar; for he who does not love his brother whom he has seen, how can he love God whom he has not seen? And this commandment we have from Him: that he who loves God must love his brother also." Loving our brothers and sisters means giving water to the thirsty, feeding the hungry, caring for the sick, and clothing the naked. (Matthew 25:34-40 NIV). To love means caring for those in need.

God's love is about action. Your love of God should be a call to action. In the book of James, Chapter 2, we are called to express our faith through our actions. James 2:14 (NIV) says, "What good is it my brothers and sisters, if someone claims to have faith but has no deeds? Can such faith save them?" Verse 17 (NIV) says, "Faith by itself, if it is not accompanied by action, is dead." So, God wants you to show your love for Him through your actions and your good deeds. Your good deeds should be the expression of your love for God. If you love God, it is now time for you to roll up your sleeves and get to work! God has a job for you. You will learn what that work is through prayer and through your intimate relationship with the Holy Spirit.

God's call to love our brothers and sisters is not limited to our brothers and sisters in Christ. God calls us to love all people—not just those who look like us or think as we think. Unfortunately, our society and our culture have made us fearful of those who don't look like we do, don't talk like we talk, don't think like we think, or value the same things that we value. If you truly love God and are in relationship with Him, it is easier to look past these differences. As humans, we all have the same basic needs of food, clothing, shelter, and a desire to love and be loved by other people in this world. History has taught us over and over again that nothing good comes from hating our brothers or sisters. To love like God, we must look past our differences and embrace our similarities.

It is only when we start to value each other as human beings and truly love our neighbors as ourselves that this world will become a better place. It is only when we love each other unconditionally that we can advance as a human race. Think of how different the world would be if we truly cared for our brothers and sisters the way God wants us to care for each other. There would be no hunger, no homelessness, and no poverty. Being in right relationship with God is not only about loving God, it's also about loving the people in the world. We can express our love of God through our actions, whether those actions are great or whether those actions are small. Expressing that love can be as simple as a kind word to a stranger or making a huge sacrifice to help someone in need. Jesus tells us in John 13:35 (NIV), "By this everyone will know that you are my disciples, if you love one another."

There is a quote that is attributed to the theologian John Wesley that sums up God's call to action very well:

> Do all the good you can,
> By all the means you can,
> In all the ways you can,
> In all the places you can,
> At all the times you can,
> To all the people you can,
> As long as you ever can.

How can you show God's love to someone today?

NOTES

Chapter 7

FEAR OR FAITH?

There are certainly many times on this journey that the Lord has led me into unfamiliar places. I have been taken out of my comfort zone on more than one occasion. It is a normal part of our human nature to fear the unknown. It is a strategy for self-preservation. But fear of the unknown comes with consequences. If we are afraid to venture into unknown territory, we can fail to grow and become stagnant. Growth is an important part of the salvation journey. In 2 Corinthians 5:17 (KJV), it says, "Therefore, if anyone is in Christ, he is a new creation; old things have passed away; behold, all things have become new." You cannot become the new creation God wants you to be without growth.

God is going to press you and encourage you to use your talents and abilities to their fullest extent. God wants you to grow! Your salvation journey is going to stretch you and challenge you to be the best that you can be for God. There is going to be a struggle between your fear of the unknown and your faith in God. There are examples of this fear versus faith struggle throughout the Bible. One story that I find most memorable is in the book of Numbers, Chapters 13 and 14. It tells the story of the people of Israel getting ready to receive a great promise from God. God promised the people of Israel the land of Canaan as an inheritance, but the land was already occupied by other people.

The people of Israel sent spies to explore the land before they took possession of it as God had promised them. Moses chose twelve spies, one from each tribe, to go and explore the land. They were tasked to explore the type of soil, the trees, the people, and the cities in the land that God had promised them. When the spies returned, they gave their report to Moses that the land that God had promised them "does flow with milk and honey" (Numbers 13: 27, NIV). But they also reported that the people who lived in the land were powerful and lived in large, fortified cities (Numbers 13:28). The people of the land were giants, and the people of Israel were afraid of them (Numbers 13:32). Some of the spies described themselves as grasshoppers. "We seemed like grasshoppers in our own eyes, and we looked the same to them." (Numbers 13:33) The people even cried out to Moses that they should have died in Egypt or maybe it would have been better for them to go back to Egypt and be slaves (Numbers 14:2-4).

But two of the spies, Caleb and Joshua, urged the people not to be afraid to take possession of the land because God was with them.

> The land we passed through and explored is exceedingly good. If the Lord is pleased with us, he will lead us into that land, a land flowing with milk and honey, and will give it to us. Only do not rebel against the Lord. And do not be afraid of the people of the land, because we will devour them. Their protection

is gone, but the Lord is with us. Do not be afraid of them. (Numbers 14:7-9, NIV)

The people of Israel did not like the report of Caleb and Joshua and wanted to stone them, but God showed up in the middle of the meeting. God was angry with the people of Israel for being afraid to take possession of the land He had promised them. "The Lord said to Moses, 'How long will these people treat me with contempt? How long will they refuse to believe in me, in spite of all the signs I have performed among them?'" (14:11). God had already brought the people of Israel out of slavery in Egypt, protected them from Pharaoh's army with a pillar of cloud by day and a pillar of fire by night, and allowed them to escape Pharaoh's army by crossing the Red Sea on dry land.

Like most of us, the people of Israel had a fear-versus-faith moment. The people of Israel chose to let their fear win. Despite all that God had brought them through, they chose to believe what they saw with their eyes (the giant people in the land) rather than believe what God promised them. Caleb and Joshua, on the other hand, chose to believe God's promises even when others saw impossibility. Caleb and Joshua were walking by faith and not by sight. The people of Israel were asked to leave the familiar for the unfamiliar. They could see this great promise right before them, but they were afraid. Sound familiar?

God knew He was asking the people of Israel to do something difficult. He repeatedly encouraged them to be strong and courageous and that He would be with them. Moses told the people of Israel in Deuteronomy 7:17-19 (NIV):

You may say to yourselves, "These nations are stronger than we are. How can we drive them out?" But do not be afraid of them; remember well what the Lord your God did to Pharaoh and to all Egypt. You saw with your own eyes the great trials, the signs and wonders, the mighty hand and outstretched arm, with which the Lord your God brought you out.

And in Deuteronomy 1:29-30, "Then I said to you, 'Do not be terrified; do not be afraid of them. The Lord your God, who is going before you, will fight for you, as he did for you in Egypt, before your very eyes." If they had just been obedient to God, they would have been blessed beyond measure. The land flowing with milk and honey would have been theirs! Because of their disobedience, God punished the people of Israel, and they were forced to wander in the desert for forty years. Only Caleb and Joshua would enter the Promised Land.

Despite their disobedience, God did not deny the people of Israel their inheritance of the Promised Land. He just delayed the promise for forty years until a more obedient generation of people were willing to put their faith into action. Moses handed leadership over to Joshua. But before doing so, Moses encouraged Joshua and told him, "Be strong and courageous. Do not be afraid or terrified because of them, for the Lord your God goes with you; he will never leave you nor forsake you" (Deuteronomy 31:6, NIV).

So, no matter where you find yourself on this journey, remember that God is always there with you. Sometimes, it will be very evident that God is present and working miracles in ways that only God can do. But as you grow and mature as a Christian, you will be able to tackle more difficult assignments. You won't always need God to hold your hand to complete the tasks that He has assigned to you. I often tell people it is when you look back over your life that you can see God's handiwork. When I look back over my life, I can see the struggles and challenges that God has brought me through. But I have also had situations where I can see God's miraculous work in the here and now.

Even the disciples had the fear-or-faith struggle. Mark 4:35-41 (NKJV) tells the story of the disciples' struggle with their fear. The disciples were in the boat with Jesus, and they were going to the other side of the lake when a furious storm came about. The wind whipped the waves, and the boat began to take on water. Jesus was asleep in the stern of the boat when the disciples woke him and asked, "Teacher, do You not care that we are perishing?" (Mark 4:38 NKJV). Jesus responded by calming the wind and the sea. "Then He arose and rebuked the wind, and said to the sea, 'Peace, be still!' And the wind ceased and there was a great calm." But that is not the end of the story. Jesus brings to the disciples' attention their lack of faith. "But he said to them, 'Why are you so fearful? How is it that you have no faith?' And they feared exceedingly, and said to one another, 'Who can this be, that even the wind and the sea obey Him!'" (Mark 4:39-41, NKJV). So, even the disciples who walked with Jesus had the fear versus faith struggle. You will have this struggle as well.

I can remember the first fear-or-faith challenge that I faced. It was 2004, less than a year after my son's accident. I had returned to my private group practice, but I felt like I just didn't belong there any longer. My husband and I had multiple discussions about what the best option would be for my career. We even talked about opening my own private practice, which was something I was never interested in doing. I never wanted to be the boss. I considered myself a good worker bee, but I had no interest in running the hive. But God had other ideas for me. I struggled with the decision. It was clear to me I could not stay where I was, but I was afraid of starting my own practice. How could I handle the challenges of running my own practice and caring for my daughters and my severely handicapped son?

And then one day God spoke to me. It is still a vivid memory for me. I was running errands in my husband's truck. I needed to pick up some medical supplies for my son, and I stopped at the local medical supply store. I was getting back in the truck when God spoke to me, and these were His words: "If you trust me as much as you say you do, then do this." I knew what "this" was. It had been on my mind for days. God wanted me to use my newly found faith and start my own practice.

I said, "Okay, God." It's kind of hard to argue with God when He uses your own words against you. I talked it over with my husband. He was one hundred percent in agreement, and I turned in my resignation. I then began the difficult task of opening my own practice. And God was with me every step of the way—from meeting multiple deadlines to open the practice on schedule, to providing much-needed rest after working thirty-six hours straight.

When I look back over the time I spent in my private practice, I see God weaved throughout the whole practice. I think about the lives I was able to touch because I said yes to God and rejected my fears. Building my practice strengthened my own faith and allowed me to share my faith with a multitude of people. It also allowed me to show

God's love to a variety of people, many of whom, needed to experience God's love.

Another fear-or-faith challenge came with writing this book. I have never thought of myself as a writer and certainly not an author. I have always been a concise, straight-to-the-point kind of writer and a woman of few words when it comes to writing. I can remember in high school and college, struggling to complete writing assignments. If the teacher or professor wanted a four-page paper, I would have three pages of information with three or four lines on the fourth page. So, the idea of writing a whole book was daunting. But here I am writing a book, and once again, God has been with me every step of the way. The book began as notes I made after prayer sessions. I got in the habit of writing down God's answers to my prayers. Sometimes the answers were for me; sometimes the answers were meant to be shared with others. This book is the result. But even after I completed the manuscript, I wrestled with whether to publish it. There are thousands of books about salvation, written by authors far more eloquent than I am. Why would anyone be interested in what I had to say? But ultimately, it's not about me. It's about being obedient to God and allowing God to work through me.

When you feel like fear is winning, understand that God wants the best for you. One of my favorite scriptures is Romans 8:28 (NIV) which states, "And we know that in all things God works for the good of those who love him, who have been called according to his purpose." This does not mean that everything is always going to be good in your life. What it does mean is that if you love God and are in relationship with Him, some good can come out of every situation if you allow God's will to be done. Sometimes I must remind myself that no matter what I am called to do on this journey, it will work out for the good. Sometimes it is for my good, but a lot of times it is for the good of others. But either way, I am the better for it.

Yes, you are going to have the fear-or-faith struggle. The question then becomes—is your faith going to win, or is your fear going to win? The more you learn to trust God, the easier the fear-versus-faith struggle becomes. We are still going to have the struggle; but the more time you spend with God, the more you realize He will lead and guide you through your struggle. Remember no matter what you face, God is with you in the struggle. Let's look at Isaiah 43:1-2 (NIV), "But now, this is what the Lord says— he who created you, Jacob, he who formed you, Israel: 'Do not fear, for I have redeemed you; I have summoned you by name; you are mine. When you pass through the waters, I will be with you; and when you pass through the rivers, they will not sweep over you. When you walk through the fire, you will not be burned; the flames will not set you ablaze.'" This tells me that God is my protector. I have nothing to fear. When calamity comes my way, it will not destroy me because God is with me.

When your fear wins, I promise that you have missed out on something glorious that God has for you. Remember, Philippians 4:13 (NKJV) says, "I can do all things through Christ who strengthens me." That tells me that no matter what God has asked me to do, I can do it because Christ is with me. Think about your own fear or faith challenges. Did your fear win? Or did your faith win? As you grow in Christ, you will become more empowered in your faith, and your faith will help you to overcome your fear.

NOTES

Chapter 8

WHY DO BAD THINGS HAPPEN TO GOOD PEOPLE?

I feel I would be remiss if I did not at least attempt to answer the question—why do bad things happen to good people? On my Christian journey, there is one thing that I have found to be quite interesting. I have found many people who have the misconception that once we become Christians, our struggles in life are over. They believe that God will take away all their problems and remove any challenges they may face in life. That is obviously not the case. Yes, sometimes God will solve our problems. However, what many fail to realize is the value in the day-to-day struggles that life brings.

I also think that when bad or tragic things happen in people's lives, it can become a source of anger with God if they don't understand why. Being saved does not exclude you from the problems that come along with being a human being. There will be sickness, death, hunger, loneliness, and times of desperation that are part of being human. It is in the struggles of life that we build our strength, find courage, learn patience, develop endurance, and build faith. Entering into a relationship with

God gives us the hope that things will get better and the strength to endure until they do.

So why do bad things happen to good people? This question has been plaguing humanity for centuries. If God is good, why does He allow bad things to happen? Why is there illness, murder, war, hunger, and poverty? I do not claim to be a theologian, nor do I claim to have all the answers. One of the things we need to understand is that the world we live in is not fair or just. For me, the answer to the question—why do bad things happen to good people?—involves free will, sin, and the limited understanding we have of God. God allows us to choose how we will live and the decisions we make in life. We have the choice to accept God and aspire to live a righteous life, or we can reject God and choose to live in sin. But as humans, we also have a limited understanding of God's wisdom, power, and authority.

That leads us to a discussion of sin and the consequences of sin. Sin, as defined by the *Bible Doctrine: Essential Teachings of the Christian Faith*, is "any failure to conform to the moral law of God in act, attitude, or nature."[4] We can have sinful thoughts, sinful desires, and sinful actions. All of these are contrary to the moral law of God, and all separate us from God. God hates sin as much as He loves us. Sin is absolutely a contradiction to the moral character and nature of God. God is holy and will not tolerate or ignore sin. It is because of sin that evil and bad things exist in the world.[5]

There are consequences of sin. One consequence of sin is death. Paul tells us in Romans 6:23 "For the wages of sin is death." The death that Paul speaks of is eternal separation from God. Proverbs 10:16 tells us, "The earnings of the wicked are sin and death." Not only does sin lead to death, but it is also harmful to us. With sin comes destruction, pain, and suffering. But ultimately, the greatest consequence of unresolved sin is separation from God. In addition to separation from God, those who reject God will earn eternal torment.

In the creation story in Genesis, the Bible tells us that everything that God made was good, including the light, the land, the seas, the vegetation, the stars, the creatures of the sea, the birds, the living creatures of the land, the livestock, and the wild animals. And finally, God created mankind in His own image. Genesis 1:31 (NIV) tells us, "God saw all that he had made, and it was very good." So, if everything God made was good, where did sin come from? At the beginning of Genesis Chapter 3, we are introduced to Satan disguised as a serpent. "Now the serpent was more crafty than any of the wild animals the Lord God had made" (Genesis 3:1 NIV). There is no explanation given at this time of where the serpent came from or who the serpent really was. The serpent enticed Eve and eventually Adam to sin. As we continue in Chapter 3, we see the serpent's motives were to get Adam and Eve to doubt God's goodness and to question God's authority.

But sin was present before Adam and Eve. Sin entered Creation when one of God's angels became full of pride and decided he no longer wanted to serve God. Like humans, angels are created beings that are a part of the universe God created. They are spiritual beings with moral judgment and intelligence but lack physical bodies. Angels were designed to serve God, but they can choose to serve God, or they can choose to reject God.[6] Sin entered God's creation when angels willfully chose to rebel against God and defy the very nature of God. Satan was originally one of God's angels. But Satan was not just any angel; he apparently was the model of perfection. The passage in Ezekiel 28:12-18 (NIV) is interpreted by modern-day biblical scholars as a description of the fall of Satan:

> You were the model of perfection, full of
>   wisdom and perfect in beauty.
> You were in Eden, the garden of God; every
>   precious stone adorned you: carnelian,
>   chrysolite and emerald, topaz, onyx, and
>   jasper, lapis lazuli, turquoise and beryl.
> Your settings and mountings were made of
>   gold; on the day you were created they
>   were prepared.
> You were anointed as a guardian cherub, for so
>   I ordained you.
> You were on the holy mount of God; you
>   walked among the fiery stones.
> You were blameless in your ways from the day
>   you were created till wickedness was
>   found in you.
> Through your widespread trade you were filled
>   with violence, and you sinned.
> So I drove you in disgrace from the mount
>   of God, and I expelled you, guardian
>   cherub, from among the fiery stones.
> Your heart became proud on account of your
>   beauty, and you corrupted your wisdom
>   because of your splendor.
> So I threw you to the earth; I made a spectacle
>   of you before kings.
> By your many sins and dishonest trade you
>   have desecrated your sanctuaries.

> So I made a fire come out from you, and it
> consumed you, and I reduced you to
> ashes on the ground in the sight of all
> who were watching.

Satan was not just any angel but a cherub. Cherubs are angels with close proximity to God and are responsible for guarding His holiness. Satan may have been a part of the inner courts of heaven.[7] Isaiah 14:13-14 (NIV) is also felt to describe the fall of Satan and attributes this fall to pride. "You said in your heart, 'I will ascend to the heavens; I will raise my throne above the stars of God; I will sit enthroned on the mount of assembly, on the utmost heights of Mount Zaphon. I will ascend above the tops of the clouds; I will make myself like the Most High.'" So, it was pride and a desire to be greater than God that led to Satan's fall and destruction. The fire from within described in Ezekiel is felt to be the fire of rebellion.

As we see in the fall of Satan, sin was already present in God's creation even before Adam and Eve sinned.[8] Originally, the relationship between God and humankind was perfect. God made man in His own image and supplied him with a helpmate. He designed a perfect place for them to live with everything they needed. God also gave them the opportunity to choose whether they would follow His commands or make their own decisions about how they would live. When God created Adam, He commanded Adam, "You are free to eat from any tree in the garden; but you must not eat from the tree of the knowledge of good and evil, for when you eat from it you will certainly die" (Genesis 2:16-17 NIV).

Then, along came the serpent who enticed Eve to eat the fruit of the tree of the knowledge of good and evil. It was humans in willful disobedience to God that brought the consequences of sin to mankind. And that is when humankind's relationship with God was damaged. It is when Eve gave in to temptation that sin becomes a part of human history. She saw that the fruit was "good for food and pleasing to the eye, and also desirable for gaining wisdom" (Genesis 3:6 NIV). So, she ate it and gave some to Adam as well. It is Satan's deception of Eve that introduces sin to humanity. Adam and Eve were kicked out of the Garden of Eden, and that is the beginning of the human condition in a damaged relationship with God. Since that time, God has been giving humankind the opportunity to restore that relationship with Him.

First John 3:8 (NIV) tells us Satan has been sinning since the beginning. "The one who does what is sinful is of the devil, because the devil has been sinning from the beginning. The reason the Son of God appeared was to destroy the devil's work." Satan is an evil angel who sinned and rebelled against God and now continually perpetuates evil in the world. Satan will use deception, discouragement, diversion, defeat, and delay to turn people away from God and destroy themselves (John 8:44; Revela-tion 12:9; 2 Corinthians 4:4).[9] It is when we choose sin that we continue to perpetuate evil and bad things in the world. Some things exist in the world because we allow them to exist. We choose to allow poverty, hunger, hatred, discrimination, and homelessness to exist. We have decided that it is more important to accumulate wealth than to help our brothers and sisters in need. Once sin entered the world, it will continue to exist until Jesus finally puts an end to sin forever. Revelation 20:14 (NIV) states, "Then death and Hades were thrown into the lake of fire." Anything wicked—Satan, the beast, the false prophet, demons, death, Hades, and anyone whose name is not written in the Book of Life—will be destroyed.

Humanity has existed in a sinful state since the time of Adam and Eve. So why is suffering part of the human condition? When sin entered the world, suffering came along with it. The words "cursed," "pain," "painful toil," and "sweat of your brow" are the words God used after Adam and Eve had eaten from the Tree of the Knowledge of Good and Evil (Genesis 3:14-17, NIV). Suffering was the consequence of Adam and Eve choosing evil. When a person chooses evil, it impacts that person, but it can also impact the people around them, such as family, friends, or even people they don't know. Even as Christians, we will suffer. Christ suffered for us, so why do we believe that we will not suffer as well?

Accepting Jesus Christ does not mean that you will never have another crisis or stressful situation in your life. It means that God is always with you, even during the stress and turmoil in your life. In His Word, God tells us that He will never leave us nor forsake us (Deuteronomy 31:8, NIV). Even though bad things may happen, the opportunity exists for a blessing in the middle of the suffering *if* we choose to look for it. You should not ask, why is this bad thing happening to me? Instead, you should ask, what can I learn from this bad situation? It is through suffering that we can grow and change.

Romans 5:2-4 (NIV) tells us, "And we boast in the hope of the glory of God. Not only so, but we also glory in our sufferings, because we know that suffering produces perseverance; perseverance, character; and character, hope." It is through suffering that we have the hope that things will improve and develop the endurance to withstand the suffering. We can also develop improved character through suffering, which should in turn promote more hope. Let's look at it this way: in the middle of the trials and tribulations of life, we always hope that things will get better. And if your faith in God gets you through that difficult situation, you develop endurance. The hope and endurance get you ready for the next challenge you will face in life. Prayerfully, your hope will continue to grow with every trial you face. Suffering can be a tool to becoming a better person if we see it as a tool. Suffering can also help you to trust God once you realize that God can get you through any situation in life.

Just to be clear, God is not the author of evil in our world. Bad things happen because we have a choice between good and evil in the world. With the opportunity for good comes the opportunity for evil. We as human beings need to accept responsibility for the evil that exists in the world. We need to accept responsibility for our sins, but *sin should not rule* over us. God calls us to rule over sin.

In Genesis Chapter 4, Cain was jealous of his brother, Abel. Abel provided a sacrifice that was pleasing to God, but God was not pleased with Cain's sacrifice. Cain grew jealous and angry with his brother. But the Lord warned Cain about sin. Genesis 4:6-7 (NLT) says, "Why are you so angry?" the Lord asked Cain. "Why do you look so dejected? You will be accepted if you do what is right. But if you refuse to do what is right, then watch out! Sin is crouching at the door, eager to control you. But you must subdue it and be its master." Sin still lurks outside our door today, and we must overcome it. We are not expected to do this alone. It is by the power of the Holy Spirit that we overcome sin.

However, sin and free will only partially answer the question, why do bad things happen to good people? To provide additional insight into this question, we need to look at the book of Job. The book of Job describes the suffering of Job, a righteous man who had found favor with God. In Job 1:1 (NIV), Job is identified as "blameless and upright; he feared God and shunned evil." In a conversation with God, Satan implies that if goodness is always rewarded, it is impossible to know if the goodness comes from loving God or from loving the things that God can provide. God is pleased with Job's character and his lifestyle. But Satan contends that the only reason Job fears the Lord is that the Lord has placed a hedge of protection around Job and blessed Job with great wealth. So, God allows Satan to inflict suffering on Job, but with some limitations. In a very short period of time, Job lost everything he owned, and all his children were killed. And if that was not enough, God allowed Satan to attack his health, and Job was afflicted with painful sores from the top of his head to the soles of his feet.

Despite all his suffering, Job never cursed God as Satan predicted. After learning of all these calamities, Job fell to the ground and worshipped God and said, "Naked I came from my mother's womb, and naked I will depart. The LORD gave and the LORD has taken away; may the name of the Lord be praised" (Job 1:21 NIV). Much to Satan's dismay, Job did not curse God; instead, Job realizes that everything he had came from God and despite his sorrow and pain, he offered praise to God. In fact, Job was willing to accept both the good and the bad that happen in life. He states in 2:10 (NIV), "Shall we accept good from God, and not trouble?"

Job had three friends Eliphaz, Bildad, and Zophar who initially tried to console and comfort him. But Job's friends assumed incorrectly that suffering is always the result of sin. They insisted that Job's suffering was the result of his sin. They tried to convince Job that the only way to end his suffering was to repent of his sins. Job argued with his friends about the cause of his suffering. Job insisted that he had done nothing to deserve the suffering he was experiencing but to no avail. Job continued to argue that he had done nothing wrong and wanted an audience with God.

When God answered Job, God asked Job question after question about the intricacies of God's creation. These were questions that Job did not have the wisdom or the understanding to answer. Job finally admitted he had a limited understanding of God's power and God's wisdom. God rebuked Job's friends for incorrectly making assumptions about God. They assumed they knew the cause of Job's suffering. God never answered Job about the cause of his suffering, but Job was eventually blessed by God with twice as much as he had before. And Job went on to live for 140 years.

Job never identified the cause of his suffering. Is the *why* in why we suffer really that important? Does knowing the *why* change the fact that we are suffering? There will always be more questions than answers in life. When questions arise, we need to seek God for guidance in life's dilemmas. It's about confidently trusting God even when we don't have all the answers because we are never going to have all the answers! Ecclesiastes 3:11 (NIV) tells us, "He has made everything beautiful in its time. He has also set eternity in the human heart; yet no one can fathom what God has done from beginning to end." We can never fully understand God, and we can never fully understand His actions. We should trust God for who He is, not merely what He can do for us.

I would like for you to consider this idea as well. When we suffer, God suffers with us. God wanted to restore the relationship with humankind so much that He sacrificed Himself through His son Jesus Christ to save us. So, even though bad things may happen to us, God is with us through it all.

So, we know that bad things happen in life. How do you respond to the bad things that happen in your life? Is it an opportunity for growth and maturation, or is it an opportunity to wallow in self-pity? Just as we know bad things will happen in life, we should also know there is an opportunity for good things to occur as a result of the bad things that happen. The opportunity for good exists if you believe it is possible for something good to come out of every bad situation.

How do we find the good? We find the good through Christ. As believers in Jesus Christ, we face the challenge of being in Christ and the struggles of being in the world. But be assured by the words of 1 John 4:4 (NIV) which tells us: "You, dear children, are from God and have overcome them, because the one who is in you is greater than the one who is in the world." The Spirit of God within you as a believer is greater than anything you will ever face in the world. The world offers struggle and conflict, but it's not about the struggle; it's about trusting God in the struggles and the conflicts that life brings. In 2 Corinthians 4:16-18 (NIV), Paul tells us:

> Therefore, we do not lose heart. Though outwardly we are wasting away, yet inwardly we are being renewed day by day. For our light and momentary troubles are achieving for us an eternal glory that far outweighs them

all. So, we fix our eyes not on what is seen, but on what is unseen, since what is seen is temporary, but what is unseen is eternal.

In other words, the pain and anguish that we go through here on earth cannot compare to the glory that God has waiting for us in eternity. So don't focus on the pain in the here and the now. Focus on Jesus and eternity. Jesus promises us sustenance and peace. Paul is encouraging us to trust in God's promise of eternal life through faith. And we are reminded that even though our physical bodies are dying, our spiritual bodies are being renewed day by day.

When we focus on Jesus, we find peace. In John 14:27 (NLT), Jesus tells us, "I am leaving you with a gift—peace of mind and heart. And the peace I give is a gift the world cannot give. So don't be troubled or afraid." There is peace that can be found in the midst of your struggles. That peace is found in Jesus Christ! Philippians 4:6-7 (NIV) says, "Do not be anxious about anything, but in every situation, by prayer and petition, with thanksgiving, present your requests to God. And the peace of God, which transcends all understanding, will guard your hearts and your minds in Christ Jesus." It is God's peace that has gotten me through the many struggles in my life.

I think about the many life and death struggles that our son, Jayden, has faced in his time here on earth. At nineteen years old, Jayden had surgery to revise his feeding tube. A couple of days after surgery, he had massive bleeding in his intestines that required him to be rushed to the emergency department. He lost half of the blood in his body and received three units of blood and needed another procedure to get the bleeding to stop. In the middle of a pandemic, he spent two days in the hospital in an ICU filled with COVID patients. Despite the stressful nature of the situation, I've learned to trust God in the midst of Jayden's struggles and in the midst of my own struggles, as well. Because God has shown me over and over that He is trustworthy, and He will take care of us. So even though it looks like chaos all around, I can rest in the peace that Jesus has promised me. I've stopped worrying about the outcome, and I've learned to focus on God.

The question becomes—are you going to focus on your problems or are you going to focus on God? We all know what happens when we focus on our problems. We end up with sleepless nights, high blood pressure, anxiety, and ulcers. Jesus tells us in John 16:33 (NIV) "I have told you these things, so that in me you may have peace. In this world you will have trouble. But take heart! I have overcome the world." Jesus was speaking to his disciples just before His arrest and crucifixion. He was telling them about His impending death and the tribulations they were about to face. He did not tell them these things to make them anxious, instead, He was offering a message of peace and hope. The world would not be kind to them. The disciples needed to know that peace could be found in Jesus, and if He was victorious, they would be victorious as well.

Jesus came to the earth so that we could live an abundant life through Him. Jesus brought a message of love, hope, and peace which could be found through a relationship with Him. The world opposed Jesus and His message, but Jesus won the victory over the world. We are to remember that Jesus has overcome the world, and we are to rejoice in this fact. "Take heart" from John 16:33 comes from the Greek word *tharseó,* which means "be courageous, cheer up".[10] Because Jesus is victorious, in union with Him, we can be victorious too. I like the way the *New Living Translation* puts it in Romans 8:35, 37-38 (NLT):

> Can anything ever separate us from Christ's love? Does it mean he no longer loves us if we have trouble or calamity, or are persecuted, or hungry, or destitute, or in danger, or threatened with death? No, despite all these things, overwhelming victory is ours through Christ, who loved us. And I am convinced that nothing can ever separate us from God's love. Neither death nor life, neither angels nor demons, neither our fears for today nor our worries about tomorrow—not even the powers of hell can separate us from God's love.

The struggles of life don't end just because you are a Christian. And just because bad things happen and we face difficulties in life, it doesn't mean that God doesn't love us. It is because God loves us that He sent His Son, Jesus Christ, so we can be victorious in our struggles. It is about having the confident hope that God will never leave you nor forsake you—no matter what comes your way. It is through Jesus Christ that you can be victorious in the bad times in life. Being victorious is about having hope and trusting God. It's understanding that being victorious means that even when bad things happen, you can become stronger, wiser, and more courageous; that you can find peace and strengthen your faith. In the end, it's about using the things that happen in life, good or bad, to become more like Jesus Christ.

Romans 8:28 (NIV) reminds us, "And we know that in all things God works for the good of those who love him, who have been called according to his purpose." Understand there are a few conditions we must meet to receive the divine blessings of God. First, we must love God and be in relationship with Him. And in that love and relationship, we find there is hope for better things. With that hope, comes the opportunity for good things to happen in our lives no matter how bad the situation may seem. No one wants to suffer or have bad things happen in their life. But when bad things happen, understand it is an opportunity to learn something, to grow as a human being, and become a better person.

As human beings, many of us do not change unless we are forced to change. It is the bad things that motivate us to change. However, this requires us to see the bad as an opportunity for growth and change. Romans 8:18 (NIV) states, "I consider that our present sufferings are not worth comparing with the glory that will be revealed in us." Our suffering can be an opportunity to reveal the glory of God that is within us. God knows the potential that is within each and every one of us. It is the obstacles and challenges we face in life that uncover the potential that is present within us. Not all suffering is bad because for the people of God suffering can lead to emotional and spiritual growth. I doubt very seriously I would have ever written this book had I not found myself in relationship with God. It was my son's accident that allowed me to recognize and remove the obstacles that prevented me from developing a true relationship with God. In the end, it was a bad event in my life that led to the most beautiful thing in my life—a relationship with God Almighty!

Salvation

What change have you seen in your life after a bad or even tragic event? Did the incident drive you away from God or draw you closer to God?

NOTES

Chapter 9

SHARING WHAT YOU HAVE LEARNED

The natural progression of your relationship with God is to share what you have learned with others. First, you learn about God. Then, you learn to trust God, love God, and eventually begin to love others as God loves. Ultimately, you need to share the benefits of a relationship with God with others. It's about sharing your faith. Jesus commands his followers to teach others about Him and His way of life. I like the way the *Message Bible* explains it in Matthew 28:18–20 which says:

> Jesus, undeterred, went right ahead and gave his charge: "God authorized and commanded me to commission you: Go out and train everyone you meet, far and near, in this way of life, marking them by baptism in the threefold name: Father, Son and Holy Spirit. Then instruct them in the practice of all I have commanded you. I'll be with you as you do this, day after day after day, right up to the end of the age."

Jesus is calling us to be witnesses. Being a witness means you accept the teachings of Jesus Christ and are willing to share those teachings with others. So, what does it take to be a witness? First, you must learn about God and be in relationship with Him. Being a witness requires an understanding of Jesus' teachings and a willingness to put those principles into practice in your life. Witnessing to others about Jesus Christ requires maturity in your faith and continues the cycle that Jesus commands of us in Matthew 28:18-20. Jesus never meant for us to keep what we've learned to ourselves. As we grow in Christ, we become better equipped to share the teachings of Jesus with others. Teaching others doesn't require us to be perfect, but it does require us to be in right relationship with God. We must be mature in our faith to teach others. Different people will arrive at maturity at different times in their salvation journey.

Sharing your experiences about God with others is not always easy. We have an inherent fear of being rejected. Sharing my experiences about God has never been easy for me, either. Talking about God can be a difficult conversation, especially if you don't know someone very well. It is easier to discuss God and how to have a relationship with God when you know someone. Let them *see* the difference God has made in your life, and then you can *talk* about the difference God has made in your life. Earnestly pray for their needs and ask God to present an opportunity to bring up the benefits of a relationship with Him. The decision to enter into a relationship with God is theirs alone. Remember, they have the choice to accept God or reject God. Don't be discouraged if you discuss a relationship with God, and it seems like nothing happens. Sometimes planting the seed about the possibility of a relationship with God is your only job. It may be much later before they decide to enter in a relationship with God. Your only job may be to make the introduction.

Another way to share what you've learned is to be a living example of the teachings of Jesus Christ. I think the biggest compliment anyone can pay me is when they tell me they see God in me, or they see the love of God in me. That is, after all, the whole idea. We should reflect God and God's love. We may be the only Bible some people will ever read. In other words, our expression of God's love may be the only contact some people will ever have with God. In Matthew 5:13-14 (NKJV), Jesus calls us "the salt of the earth" and "the light of the world." Jesus is calling us to be an example for others and to make a difference in the world in which we live. When people recognize that it is God's light that gives you the hope and the strength to make it from day to day despite your troubles, they can't help but want some of that light in their life as well.

With God's help, we should strive every day to be more and more like Jesus Christ. But in our day-to-day life, we should also try to introduce as many people as possible to God and God's love. One of the ways I try to introduce others to God is by praying with my patients. In my encounters with patients, they share a variety of problems with me. Some of their problems are physical and are the reason for their visit. At other times, their problems are emotional or spiritual or maybe I've just given them bad news. I ask if I can pray with them. Generally, the answer is yes, and I will pray with them for whatever circumstance they are dealing with. Occasionally the answer is no, but that doesn't prevent me from praying for them. I don't let one person's rejection prevent me from asking other people to pray with them. As I have said before, God gives us the right to accept

Him or reject Him, so who am I to force God on someone? God has given all of us gifts and talents that we can use to share His love with others. Pray for guidance on how to use your gifts and talents to share God's love with others.

When talking with others about a relationship with God, I generally start the conversation by mentioning how much God loves them. I don't think any of us really understand the depth of God's love for us. Most people have the misconception that they have done too many bad things in their life for God to love them. They believe they are beyond saving, but nothing could be further from the truth. God loves us unconditionally and wants to be in relationship with us. Paul tells us in Romans 5:8 (NLT) about God's love for us. "But God showed his great love for us by sending Christ to die for us while we were still sinners." Even though we may have done some bad things that doesn't mean we are not worthy of being in a relationship with God. Salvation is still available to us because of God's great love for us. Truth be told, none of us will ever be good enough to be in relationship with God. It is because of Jesus' willingness to take on the sins of the whole world that we have the opportunity and the privilege to have a relationship with God. God is not interested in your past. God knows every detail of your past and still loves you and wants to be in relationship with you. Being in relationship with God is about your future, not your past.

So, start the conversation by discussing God's love. Then move on to discussing God's forgiveness. It is important to mention that we have all sinned, and we have all disappointed God at one time or another. That does not stop God from loving us or wanting to be in relationship with us. Then discuss the importance of asking forgiveness for our sins and expressing a desire to be in relationship with God through His Son, Jesus Christ. If they desire a relationship with God, lead them in prayer which can be as simple as:

> *Lord, I need You. I know that I am a sinner, and I ask Your forgiveness for my sins. Jesus, I believe that You are the Son of God; that You died on the cross for my sins; and God raised You from the dead. Jesus, I want You to be my Lord and my Savior. Help me turn from my sins and live a life that is pleasing in Your sight. Amen.*

Once they have decided to enter into a relationship with God, it's important to support them in the initial stages of that relationship. Pray for them, invite them to church, and touch base with them on a regular basis. But remember, sometimes our only job is to make the introduction. It may be someone else's job to water and cultivate the seed of faith that God has planted in their lives.

Is there someone you would like to share your faith with? Pray for an opportunity to discuss the benefits of a relationship with God through His Son, Jesus Christ.

NOTES

Chapter 10

WORSHIPING IN SPIRIT AND IN TRUTH

Loving God and loving others are important on our salvation journey. One way to express our love for God is to worship Him. My Bible dictionary defines worship as "to express praise and devotion." God wants us to worship Him in Spirit and in truth. But what does that mean? In John 4:23-24 (NIV) Jesus says, "Yet a time is coming and has now come when the true worshipers will worship the Father in the Spirit and in truth, for they are the kind of worshipers the Father seeks. God is spirit, and his worshipers must worship in the Spirit and in truth." Compare this to John 4:23-24 in the *Message Bible* which says, "It's who you are and the way you live that count before God. Your worship must engage your spirit in the pursuit of truth. That's the kind of people the Father is out looking for: those who are simply and honestly *themselves* before him in their worship. God is sheer being itself—Spirit. Those who worship him must do it out of their very being, their spirits, their true selves, in adoration." Worshiping God should come from your soul. Your worship should be an authentic representation of you and who you are. In John 14:6 (KJV), Jesus tells us, "I am the way, the truth, and the life." Jesus is the truth, and we should strive to be like Him. That is when worship becomes the expression of praise and devotion God expects from us—when we are like Jesus.

God wants our whole life to be about worshiping Him. We should worship God in our spiritual walk, our talk, and our actions. This is much more than just going to church on Sundays. This is about letting your whole life reflect God. We like to compartmentalize our lives. We have our work life, our home life, and our life with friends, acting one way at work, one way at home, and a different way with our friends. In true worship, you present one you to the world. It is the one you that God saved and cleansed of your sins. It is the one you that God has poured His Spirit into. This means that *all* aspects of your life should be in honor of God.

Romans 12:1 (NIV) says, "Therefore, I urge you, brothers and sisters, in view of God's mercy, to offer your bodies as a living sacrifice, holy and pleasing to God—this is your true and proper worship." The Old Testament describes the sacrifices of goats, sheep, and rams for the forgiveness of sins. But the blood of animals could not cleanse the people of their sins. Over time, the people of Israel began to neglect their sacrifices to God. Instead of giving God their best, they began to offer God imperfect animals for sacrifice, and that was no longer acceptable to God. But God did not withhold His best from us. His Son, Jesus Christ, became the ultimate sacrifice—a perfect sacrifice that would put an end to the need for animal sacrifices. Second Corinthians 5:21 (NLT) tells us, "For God made Christ, who never sinned, to be the offering for our sin, so that we could be made right with God through Christ." God gave His best for us. So, we should give our best to God as well. God wants your whole life to reflect His love.

Your thoughts, the words you speak, and your actions should all reflect God. This is not an easy task, but we are not expected to do this alone. God's Holy Spirit is here to help us and guide us, but only if we are willing to be led. Because our human nature is sinful and wants to cater to our fleshly desires, we need to ask God to fill us with His Spirit every day.

To worship God in spirit, we must be filled with His Spirit. Our spirit can become corrupted by the world with sins such as greed, lust, and hatred. Galatians 5:22-23 (NIV) tells us the characteristics we should expect to see when someone is filled with God's Spirit, "But the fruit of the Spirit is love, joy, peace, forbearance, kindness, goodness, faithfulness, gentleness, and self-control." When we are filled with God's Spirit, we can share God's love with other people and reflect God's Spirit back to God. God loves to recognize Himself in us. Therefore, when we worship, we should be filled with God's Spirit. It is the Spirit of God within us that connects with God in worship. It is the Spirit worshiping the Spirit. God is to be worshipped every day, not just on Sundays. And we should be filled with His Spirit every day.

To worship God in truth, we first must be truthful with ourselves. We must acknowledge and confess our sins and ask for forgiveness. We must forgive ourselves and we must forgive others. To worship God in truth, we must truly love God with every fiber of our being. And every aspect of our lives should reflect the mutual love that God has for us and we have for God. Our thoughts, our words, and our actions should reflect what we have allowed God to pour into us. You cannot give what you do not have. If we don't make much room for God, we don't have much to reflect back to God or share with others. Your whole

Worshiping in Spirit and in Truth

being and everything you say and do is meant to be a sacrifice to God.

Learning to worship God in Spirit and in truth has been a difficult part of my salvation journey. I often must remind myself that I am still on the journey. God is not through with me yet. I can see how I have grown on my journey, but I am not perfect and still fall short of my goal of being like Jesus every day. That doesn't mean I give up; it just means I get another chance to try again tomorrow. I truly love God, and I truly love my brothers and sisters on this earth. It pains me to see the hunger, the suffering, and the hatred that is so much a part of the world that we live in. If we love the way God wants us to love and let our whole lives be in worship to God, this world would be a very different place.

How can you worship God today? What can you do to express God's love?

NOTES

Chapter 11

CREATED TO SERVE

I think many of us believe salvation is solely for our own personal benefit. When God saved us, we were saved to serve God and to serve others. Ephesians 2:10 (NKJV) tells us, "For we are His workmanship, created in Christ Jesus for good works, which God prepared beforehand that we should walk in them." In this second chapter of Ephesians, Paul is speaking about the gift of salvation. Paul is clear to point out that it is not our works that save us, but it is because of God's grace and through faith that we are saved. Salvation is not from man or by man's works. Salvation is God's workmanship.[11] The Greek word used here for workmanship is *poiēma*, which denotes a work of art or a masterpiece.[12] All of creation—heaven, earth, and everything in it are God's masterpiece, and we are a part of the marvelous work that God has created. Salvation is also part of God's work of art. The purpose of salvation is transformation. We are to become more and more like Jesus Christ and in doing so, perform the good works God has planned for us. God's masterpiece of salvation is not achieved by good works, but good works should be a result of our salvation.[13] James 2:26 (NKJV) reminds us that, "For as the body without the spirit is dead, so faith without works is dead also."

God has prepared tasks and assignments for us. He expects good works from us. Paul explains the purpose of these works that God has prepared is for us to walk in them. God has prepared a path of good works for believers, which God will perform in them and through them as they walk in faith. As believers, we are to make ourselves available for these good works. In other words, we are to make ourselves available to serve.

We are created to serve, and God has given all of us talents, gifts, and abilities to complete the tasks and assignments He has given us. We find our greatest joy in life when we use the talents, gifts, and abilities we have been blessed with to serve God. First Peter 4:10-11 (NIV) reveals, "Each of you should use whatever gift you have received to serve others, as faithful stewards of God's grace in its various forms … If anyone serves, they should do so with the strength God provides, so that in all things God may be praised through Jesus Christ." That is to say, we should use our talents and abilities to glorify God.

We are created to serve, but God expects our service to be different from what the world expects of service. It's about serving God and serving others, not our own self-interests. God calls us to serve in season and out of season, whether we are liked or disliked, respected, or disrespected, and whether His message is well received or rejected. We must remember, ultimately, it is God that we are serving and not people. Ephesians 6:7-8 (NIV) reminds us, "Serve wholeheartedly, as if you were serving the Lord, not people, because you know that the Lord will reward each one for whatever good they do." God has a path of good works that He has set out in front of believers. By faith, we are to walk along that path being led by the Holy Spirit and complete the good works God has destined for us. He has given us the skills we need to complete the tasks He has assigned to us. And when we do God's work, we will receive God's reward.

True service in God's kingdom begins with humbling yourself before God and others. God wants us to serve selflessly. When we give generously with our time, our talents and our treasures, God promises to reward us generously for our efforts.

What talents, gifts, and abilities has God blessed you with? How can you use these gifts to glorify God through service?

NOTES

Chapter 12

CARING FOR YOUR SOUL

Caring for your soul is vital to the salvation journey. Salvation is more than just believing in Jesus Christ. It is about loving God, loving others, and expressing your love as a productive servant of God.

As a physician, I spend most of my day trying to improve people's health. And if I ask, most people can tell me what it means to be healthy. Most people can also tell me the things needed to maintain their health. But if I ask about spiritual health or caring for your soul, what kind of answer will you give? We spend a lot of time worrying about and tending to our physical health. We go to the doctor and take medication. Some of us eat a healthy diet, and some of us even exercise, all for the sake of our health. And for those of you who don't have any health problems, I promise you at some point in your life, you will have concerns about your health. For all the time we spend worrying about our physical health, how much consideration have we given to our spiritual health? The bodies that our souls reside in are only temporary vessels. These physical bodies that we spend so much time and energy caring for are not meant to last forever. Caring for our physical bodies is important. After all your body is the temple of the Holy

Spirit (1 Corinthians 6:19 NIV). Our souls, however, are eternal. How much time and energy do we spend preparing our souls for eternity?

The preparation for your soul's eternal journey begins here on earth. It is the things we do here on earth (or don't do) that determine the eternal fate of our soul. We will all stand before the throne of God and be judged for our actions. Jeremiah 17:10 (NIV) tells us, "I the Lord search the heart and examine the mind, to reward each person according to their conduct, according to what their deeds deserve." Revelation 20:12 (NIV) also speaks of judgment, "And I saw the dead, great and small, standing before the throne, and books were opened. Another book was opened, which is the book of life. The dead were judged according to what they had done as recorded in the books." We will be judged by our actions, but we will also be judged by our decision to accept God and aspire to live a righteous life or our decision to reject God and live in sin. Revelation 20:15 (NIV) describes the fate of those who choose to reject God, "Anyone whose name was not found written in the book of life was thrown into the lake of fire." God does not desire any of us to be thrown into the lake of fire, and He will wait patiently for us to choose. But at some point, your life on earth will come to an end, your opportunity to choose God will be gone forever, and the eternal fate of your soul will be decided.

When we choose God, it is the beginning of our soul's eternal journey with Him. Once we choose God, the work of becoming a productive and effective member of God's family begins. God has made available to us everything we need to be productive servants. Once we become part of God's family, our faith should instill in us a desire to work towards sharing our faith with others and making disciples. Second Peter 1:1-11 (NIV) tells us:

> To those who through the righteousness of our God and Savior Jesus Christ have received a faith as precious as ours:
>
> Grace and peace be yours in abundance through the knowledge of God and of Jesus our Lord.
>
> His divine power has given us everything we need for a godly life through our knowledge of him who called us by his own glory and goodness.
>
> Through these he has given us his very great and precious promises, so that through them you may participate in the divine nature, having escaped the corruption in the world caused by evil desires.
>
> For this very reason, make every effort to add to your faith goodness; and to goodness, knowledge;
>
> and to knowledge, self-control; and to self-control, perseverance; and to perseverance, godliness;
>
> and to godliness, mutual affection; and to mutual affection, love.

> For if you possess these qualities in increasing measure, they will keep you from being ineffective and unproductive in your knowledge of our Lord Jesus Christ.
>
> But whoever does not have them is nearsighted and blind, forgetting that they have been cleansed from their past sins.
>
> Therefore, my brothers and sisters, make every effort to confirm your calling and election. For if you do these things, you will never stumble,
>
> and you will receive a rich welcome into the eternal kingdom of our Lord and Savior Jesus Christ.

It is our work here on earth that prepares us for eternity in God's kingdom with Jesus Christ. God's desire is for all of us to have eternal life. But is that your desire? I don't ask that question to scare you. I ask that question to get you thinking. Are you focused on the temporary things of this world or are you focused on forever?

So, how do we prepare our soul for eternity? I compare getting our soul ready for eternity to preparing and planting a garden. Like a garden, without proper care, there will be no harvest. In the garden, the soil must be prepared before anything else can happen. The seed must be planted and watered. There needs to be the right amount of sunlight. Then the garden must be tended, or the weeds will take over or wild animals will destroy it. Our soul is much like a garden in that it must be prepared for eternity.

You must prepare your soul and the first step is being in right relationship with God by accepting Jesus Christ as your Lord and Savior. Next, you must plant the seed, which is the Word of God. That seed should be planted in your heart. It is planted in your heart by reading, studying, and memorizing the Word of God. Once the seed is planted, it needs to be watered. The Word of God is watered through prayer. Prayer gives you the opportunity to interact with God and learn more about God. It is in prayer that God speaks to you through His Word. Prayer is the key that unlocks the door to God's power in your life and to His unlimited resources. The Holy Spirit is the sunlight and the gardener that tends to the garden. The Holy Spirit is God's light within you and will transform your soul into the new creature that God wants you to be. The Holy Spirit tends to your heart and mind and helps you to avoid the sins of this world that threaten your eternal life.

Once you are in relationship with God, God's desire is for you to share your faith with others and fellowship with other believers. Worshipping God is not meant to be a solitary adventure. We are called to be the body of Christ. First Corinthians 12:12-14, 27 (NIV) tells us:

> Just as a body, though one, has many parts, but all its many parts form one body, so it is with Christ. For we were all baptized by one Spirit so as to form one body—whether Jews or Gentiles, slave or free— and we were all given the one Spirit to drink. Even so the body is not made up of one part but many. Now you are the body of Christ, and each one of you is a part of it.

Salvation

By being in fellowship with other believers, we can support one another during tests and trials, teach one another, and provide correction when necessary. Although none of us has all the talents and abilities to accomplish God's mission, together we can combine our talents and abilities to accomplish God's goals.

God has great gifts and privileges for those who believe. We are expected to use these gifts to be effective and productive believers. These gifts include redemption from sin (Romans 1:16), faith (Ephesians 2:8), peace (John 14:27), righteousness (Isaiah 61:10; 2 Corinthians 5:21), the Holy Spirit (John 14:16), and eternal life (Romans 6:23).

The ultimate gift is eternal life—the opportunity to live with God forever. I would like to focus here on the gift of faith, but faith is not a stand-alone gift. Peter tells us that there are other qualities that must be added to faith for us to be effective and productive servants. These gifts allow us to live a holy life and escape the sins of the world caused by evil desires. Living holy does not come naturally but requires the help of the Holy Spirit. Access to these gifts requires a relationship with God. God will empower and enable us, but God also requires us to learn, grow, and be obedient.

The first of the qualities to be added to faith is goodness. By goodness, Peter is referring to qualities such as honesty, integrity, and excellence. When we speak of goodness in this sense, we are speaking of the qualities that make someone a good citizen and an overall helpful individual.[14] We are reminded of the importance of doing good in Galatians 6:9-10 (NIV): "Let us not become weary in doing good, for at the proper time we will reap a harvest if we do not give up. Therefore, as we have opportunity, let us do good to all people, especially to those who belong to the family of believers." By being good to all people we can let the light of God shine in some dark places.

The second quality that should be added to faith is knowledge. This is not just any knowledge; it is the knowledge of God. It is the knowledge that is obtained from being in relationship with God and studying His Word. It is knowledge obtained through our relationship with God that enables us to determine right from wrong and to act accordingly.

Self-control should also be added to faith, but it is more than the ability to keep your emotions in check. By self-control, Peter is referring to submission to God and the Holy Spirit.[15] Galatians 5:16 (NLT) also describes self-control, "So I say, let the Holy Spirit guide your lives. Then you won't be doing what your sinful nature craves." Self-control in this instance is surrendering your will for God's perfect will. By surrendering your will for God's will, you become a more productive and effective believer because you become part of God's perfect plan.

Perseverance should also be added to faith and has been described as the "queen of virtues." Perseverance is a combination of patience, courage, and hope. The *African Bible Commentary* describes it as the "tenacity that refuses to give up when trouble comes but always looks forward to a better tomorrow."[16] Perseverance is the ability to keep going no matter how bad things may look. It is perseverance that allows us to walk by faith.

Peter continues to describe qualities that should be added to faith to make us effective and productive witnesses for Christ, and godliness is one of those qualities. The term godliness is rarely used in the New Testament because of its reference to pagan religions that were prevalent at the time the New Testament was written. Here, godliness is meant to refer to devotion or reference toward God and a practical love for our fellow human beings, especially the vulnerable and the needy.[17] We don't have the necessary resources to be godly on our own. It is through our relationship with God that we become godly. God transforms us with his Spirit into the godly creatures He desires us to be.

Another quality that should be added to faith is mutual affection. Mutual affection refers to the brotherly love we should have for one another. This is an affection that provides care and support for one another. It should be an integral part of any Christian community.[18] It is brotherly love that gives us a desire to love our neighbors as ourselves.

And last but not least, there is love. Peter is referring to the unconditional love God has for the righteous and the unrighteous.[19] God's love is an unconditional, eternal, and perfect love that we know as *agape* love. First Corinthians 13:13 tells us, "But the greatest of these is love." Love cannot be separated from faith. It is love that perfects our faith. First John 4:16 (NIV) tells us "God is love. Whoever lives in love lives in God, and God in them." That same unconditional love that God Has for us, He wants us to have for each other.

I know it can be hard to think about eternity when you are worried about how you're going to make your next mortgage or rent payment, or if you've just lost your job. Sometimes we become blinded by our troubles and forget what God has already done for us. We often lose ourselves in the temporary struggles that are part of the human condition. In the middle of our temporary struggles, we can lose sight of our eternal reward. Far too many of us are lost in the here and now. Second Corinthians 4:17-18 (NIV) reminds us, "For our light and momentary troubles are achieving for us an eternal glory that far outweighs them all. So we fix our eyes not on what is seen, but on what is unseen, since what is seen is temporary, but what is unseen is eternal."

Many of us are stuck in some past event, and we have allowed it to render us hopeless. That is not God's desire for you. God's desire is to build hope and strength and to give you the tools you need to conquer whatever may come your way. Your life on earth is temporary, but your soul is eternal. You should be preparing your soul for eternity. Don't let the temporary distractions of life interfere with the permanent fate of your soul.

Preparing for eternity is about growing in your relationship with God and becoming the new creature that God envisions you to be. God has great gifts and privileges for those who believe. The ultimate gift is eternal life. The more you get to know God, the more of Himself God can put into you. How do we care for the soul and prepare for eternal life? I believe there are six key steps in preparing for eternity.

1. Preparing for eternity begins by entering into right relationship with God by accepting Jesus Christ as your Lord and Savior. Accepting Jesus Christ as your Lord and Savior is just the beginning of your eternal journey. We must continue to grow if we want to receive "a rich welcome into the eternal kingdom of our Lord and Savior Jesus Christ" as described in 2 Peter 1:11. It is as simple as praying the following prayer: "Lord, I am a sinner, and I need you. Jesus, I realize that you died on the cross for my sins and God raised you from the dead."
2. Read, study, and memorize God's Word because it should be ingrained in your heart. It should become

a part of your spirit. This is the knowledge Peter speaks of, but we can only gain this knowledge if we seek it.

3. Pray to develop your relationship with God and activate the power of God within you. Prayer allows you to communicate with God and allows God to communicate with you. Do not underestimate the value of prayer in preparing your soul for eternity.

4. Allow yourself to have an intimate relationship with the Holy Spirit, who is meant to be a guide, a teacher, a comforter, and an advocate. It is through the Holy Spirit that you become transformed into the new creature that God calls you to be. You must let the Holy Spirit into the most private part of yourself, your soul. This requires studying God's Word, spending time with God in prayer, and tuning your heart to God's heart. We are to walk in unison with the Spirit of God. Galatians 5:25 (NIV) tells us, "Since we live by the Spirit, let us keep in step with the Spirit." We are not meant to travel this journey alone. We are meant to travel this journey with the Spirit of God. James 4:8 (NKJV) tells us, "Draw near to God and He will draw near to you." The more time you spend with God, the more time God will spend with you.

5. Love God and love everyone. Luke 10:27 (NIV) tells us, "Love the Lord your God with all your heart and with all your soul and with all your strength and with all your mind; and love your neighbor as yourself." God Himself has shown us the example of love He wants us to emulate. So, love God with every fiber of your being and love everyone else the same way. Your actions and your life should be a reflection of God's love.

6. Surrender your will for God's will. This is probably the most difficult thing we are called to do as believers. We want to tell God what to do, when to do it, and how to do it. Surrendering your will is not easy, especially when we don't understand the intricacies of God's plan. But remember, God's will is perfect, and He wants the best for you. But God's best is only available to you when you are in His will. Therefore, surrender your will to His. It is about trusting God even when we don't understand His plan. If you truly love God, you will surrender your will out of love and respect not out of fear or obligation.

The salvation journey is about the transformation God wants to bring to your life and to your soul. God wants to transform you into a marvelous new creation, a creation designed to bring glory and honor to Him. And the reward for allowing God to transform you into a new creation is to spend eternity with Him. Galatians 6:15 (NIV) tells us, "What counts is the new creation." Here Paul is reminding the Galatians that it is not about religious laws or rituals but about being transformed by God from the inside out.

It is when we invite Jesus Christ into our lives that the journey to eternal life truly begins. The salvation journey begins with accepting Jesus Christ as your Lord and Savior. But the journey shouldn't end there. The salvation journey is a journey of faith that is predicated on a personal, intimate relationship with God, being obedient to God, and loving others like God loves us. It is a journey that may take a lifetime, and it is a journey that will continue into eternity. The salvation journey promises to be the most important and amazing journey of your life.

Salvation

In closing, I leave you with the words of Paul from Philippians 1:6 (NLT), "And I am certain that God, who began the good work within you, will continue his work until it is finally finished on the day when Christ Jesus returns."

May God bless you and keep you on the journey! Amen

NOTES

NOTES

REFERENCES

A.M.E. Zion Publishing House. 1999. *The African Methodist Episcopal Zion Bicentennial Hymnal.* Charlotte: A.M.E. Zion Publishing House.

Adeyemo, Tokunboh, ed. 2006. *Africa Bible Commentary.* Grand Rapids, Michigan: The Zondervan Corporation.

Burge, Gary M. and Andrew E. Hill, ed. 2012. *The Baker Illustrated Bible Commentary.* Grand Rapids, Michigan: Baker Books.

Grudem, Wayne. 1999. *Bible Doctrine: Essential Teachings of the Christian Faith.* Grand Rapids, Michigan: Zondervan.

Walvoord, John F. and Roy B. Zuck, ed. 1983. *The Bible Knowledge Commentary: An Exposition of the Scriptures by Dallas Seminary Faculty,* Vol. 2. Colorado Springs, Colorado: David C Cook.

Walvoord, John F. and Roy B. Zuck, ed. 1985. *The Bible Knowledge Commentary: An Exposition of the Scriptures by Dallas Seminary Faculty,* Vol. 1. Colorado Springs, Colorado: David C Cook.

Zondervan. 1991. *Life Application Study Bible, New International Version.* Grand Rapids, Michigan: Zondervan.

END NOTES

1. Zondervan, *Life Application Study Bible, New International Version*. (Grand Rapids: Tyndale House Publishers and Zondervan, 2011), 2027.

2. Zondervan, *Life Application Study Bible*, 2027

3. A.M.E. Zion Publishing House, *The African Methodist Episcopal Zion Bicentennial Hymnal*. (Charlotte: A.M.E. Zion Publishing House, 1999), hymn 653.

4. Wayne Gruden, *Bible Doctrine: Essential Teachings of the Christian Faith*. (Grand Rapids: Baker Books, 2012), 210

5. Gruden, *Bible Doctrine: Essential Teachings of the Christian Faith*, 210

6. Gruden, *Bible Doctrine: Essential Teachings of the Christian Faith*, 168.

7. John Walvoord, Roy Zuck, *The Bible Knowledge Commentary: An Exposition of the Scriptures by Dallas Seminary Faculty*, Vol. 1. (Colorado Springs: David C. Cook, 1973,1978, 1984), p. 1283.

8. Gruden, *Bible Doctrine: Essential Teachings of the Christian Faith*, 176.

9. Gruden, *Bible Doctrine: Essential Teachings of the Christian Faith*, 176.

10. John Walvoord, Roy Zuck, *The Bible Knowledge Commentary: An Exposition of the Scriptures by Dallas Seminary Faculty*, Vol 2 (Colorado Springs: David C. Cook, 1973,1978, 1984), p. 330.

[11] Walvoord, Roy Zuck, *The Bible Knowledge Commentary: An Exposition of the Scriptures by Dallas Seminary Faculty*, Vol 2 (Colorado Springs: David C. Cook, 1973, 1978, 1984), p. 624

[12] Walvoord, *The Bible Knowledge Commentary: An Exposition of the Scriptures by Dallas Seminary Faculty*, Vol 2, 624

[13] Walvoord, *The Bible Knowledge Commentary: An Exposition of the Scriptures by Dallas Seminary Faculty*, Vol 2, 624

[14] Tobkunbon Adeyemo, *Africa Bible Commentary*. (Grand Rapids: The Zondervan Corporation, 2006), p 1526

[15] Adeyemo, *Africa Bible Commentary*, 1526

[16] Adeyemo, *Africa Bible Commentary*, 1526

[17] Adeyemo, *Africa Bible Commentary*, 1526

[18] Adeyemo, *Africa Bible Commentary*, 1526

[19] Adeyemo, *Africa Bible Commentary*, 1526

CPSIA information can be obtained
at www.ICGtesting.com
Printed in the USA
BVHW082022190223
658756BV00003B/744